Paisley Enchanting Designs

Detailed Beautiful Designs

ExpertAuthor BluePrint

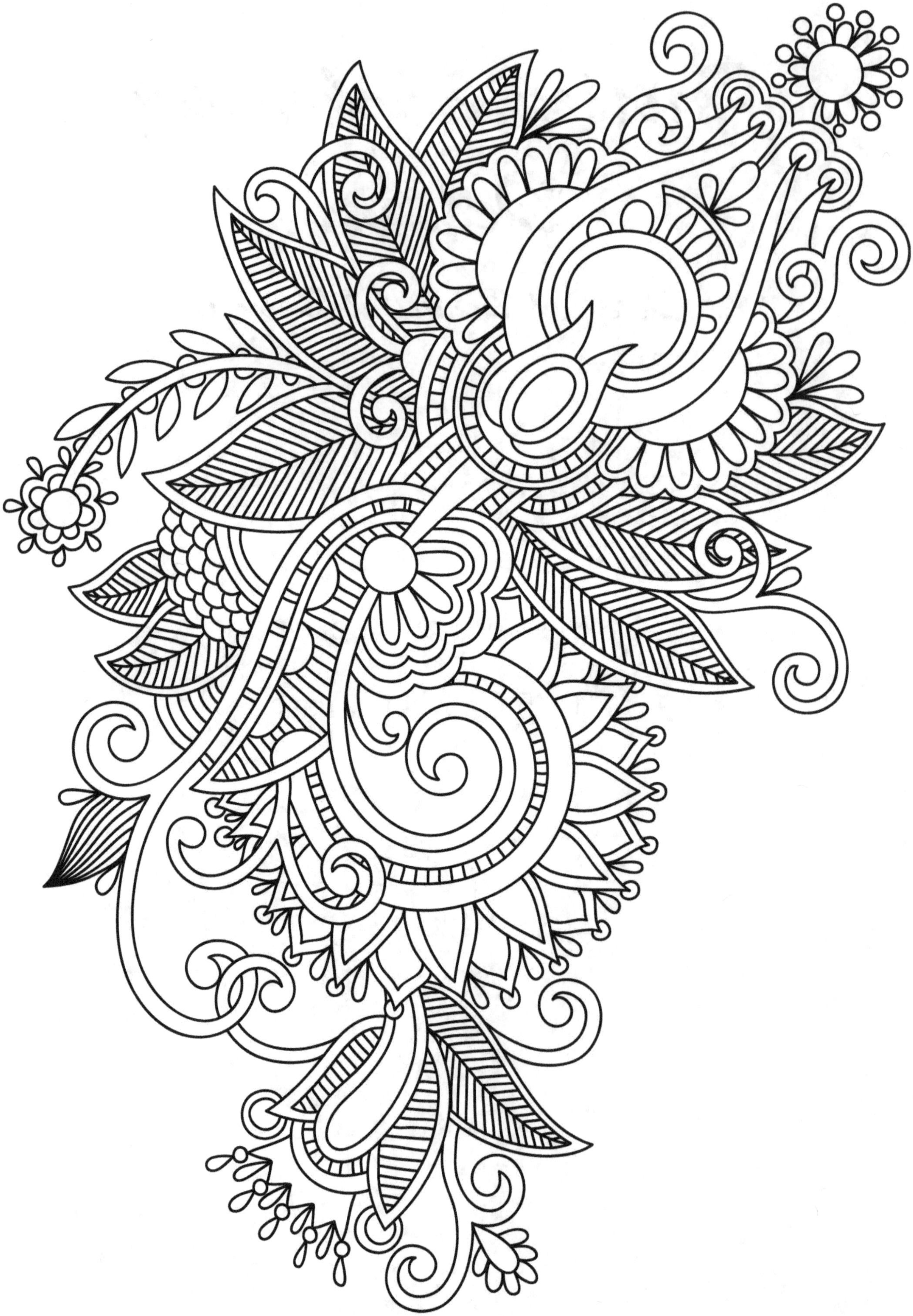

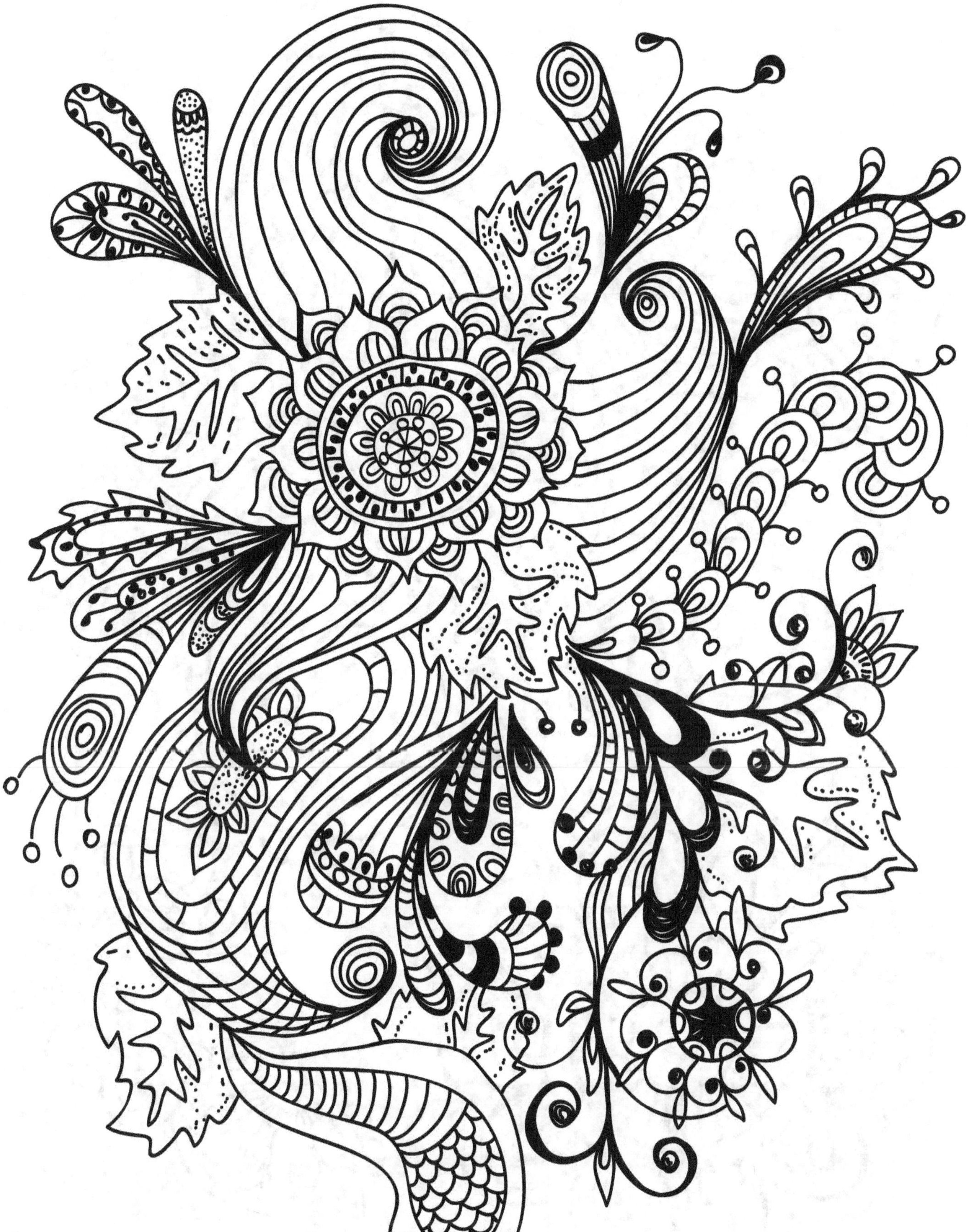

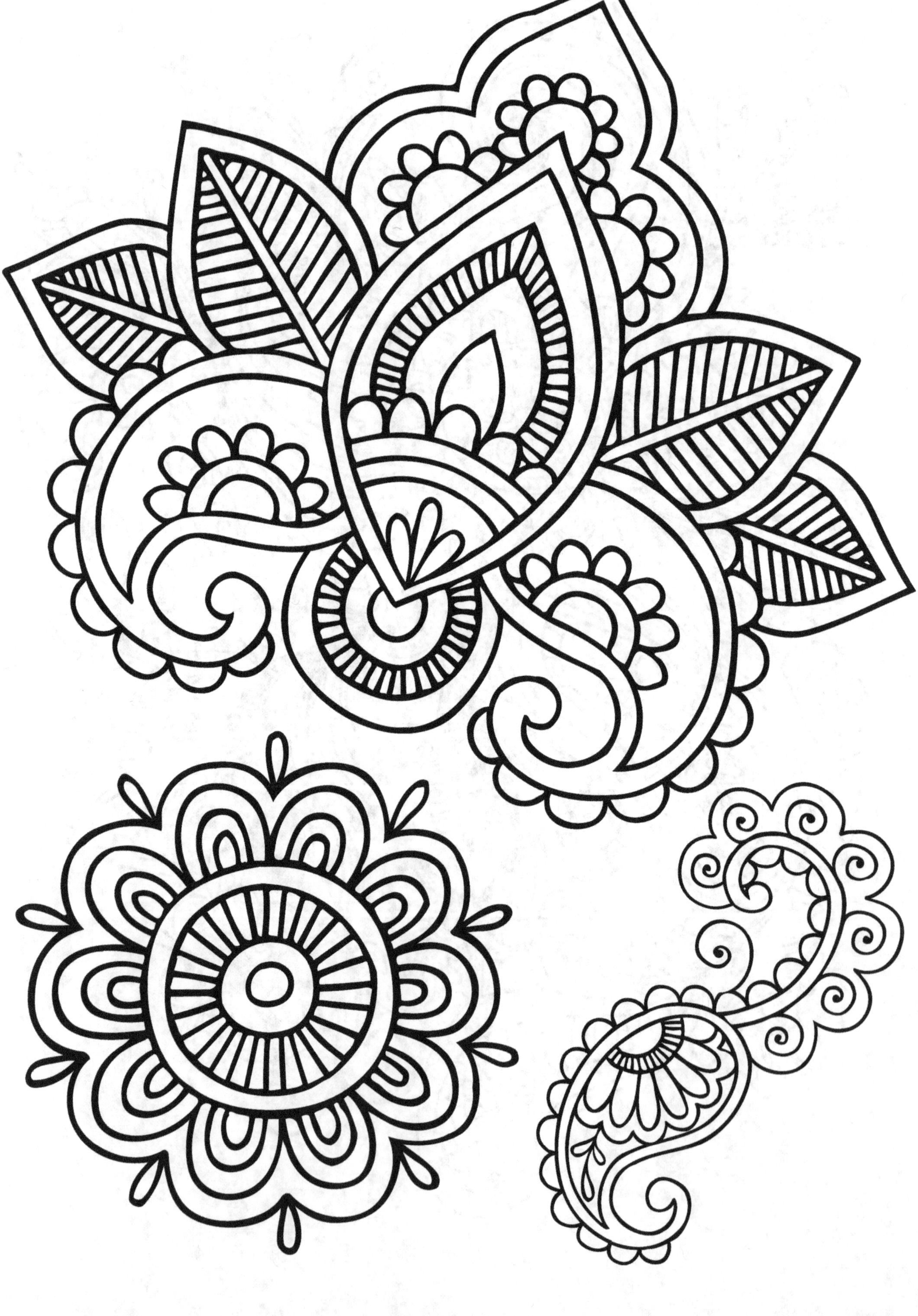

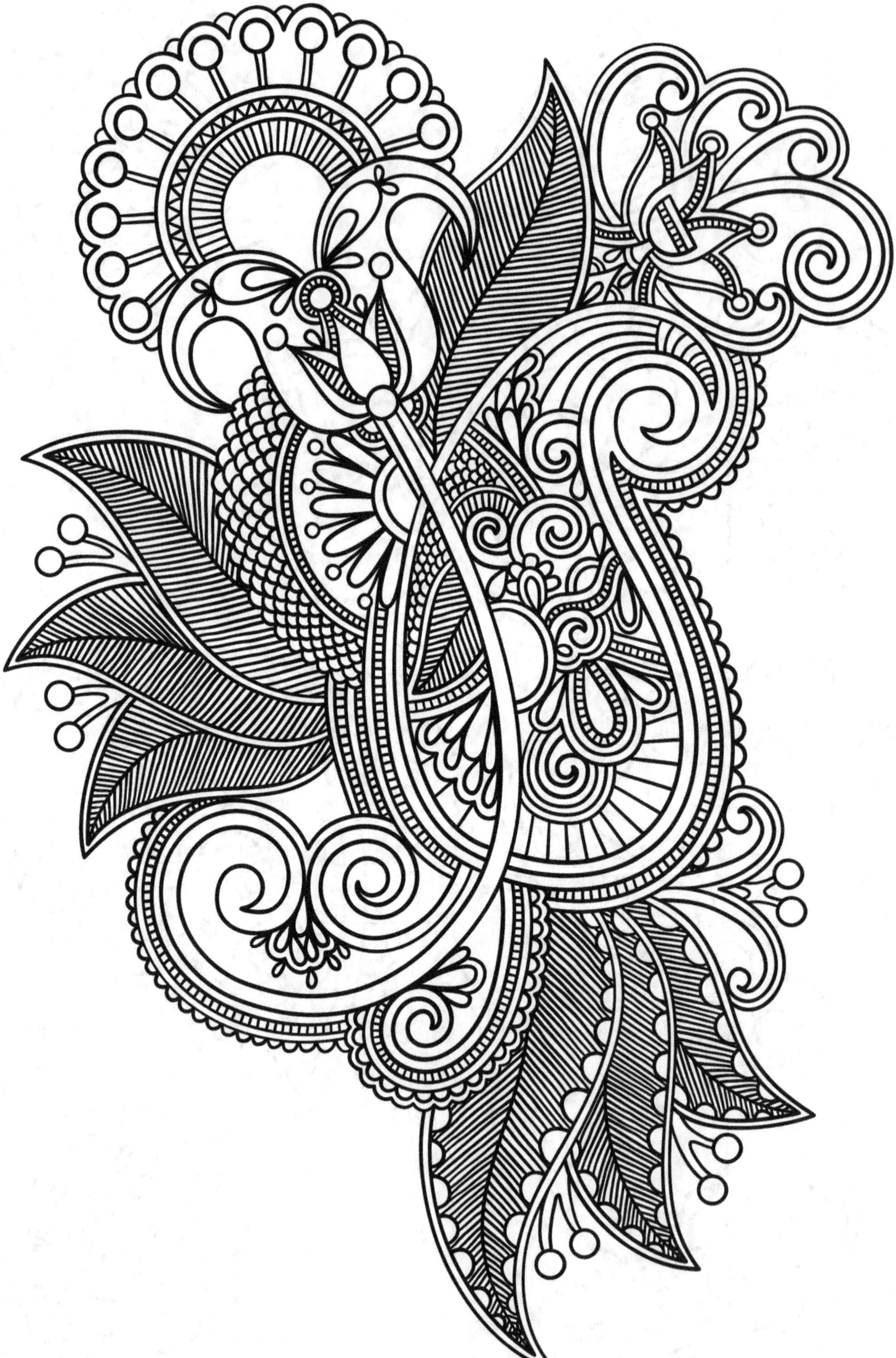

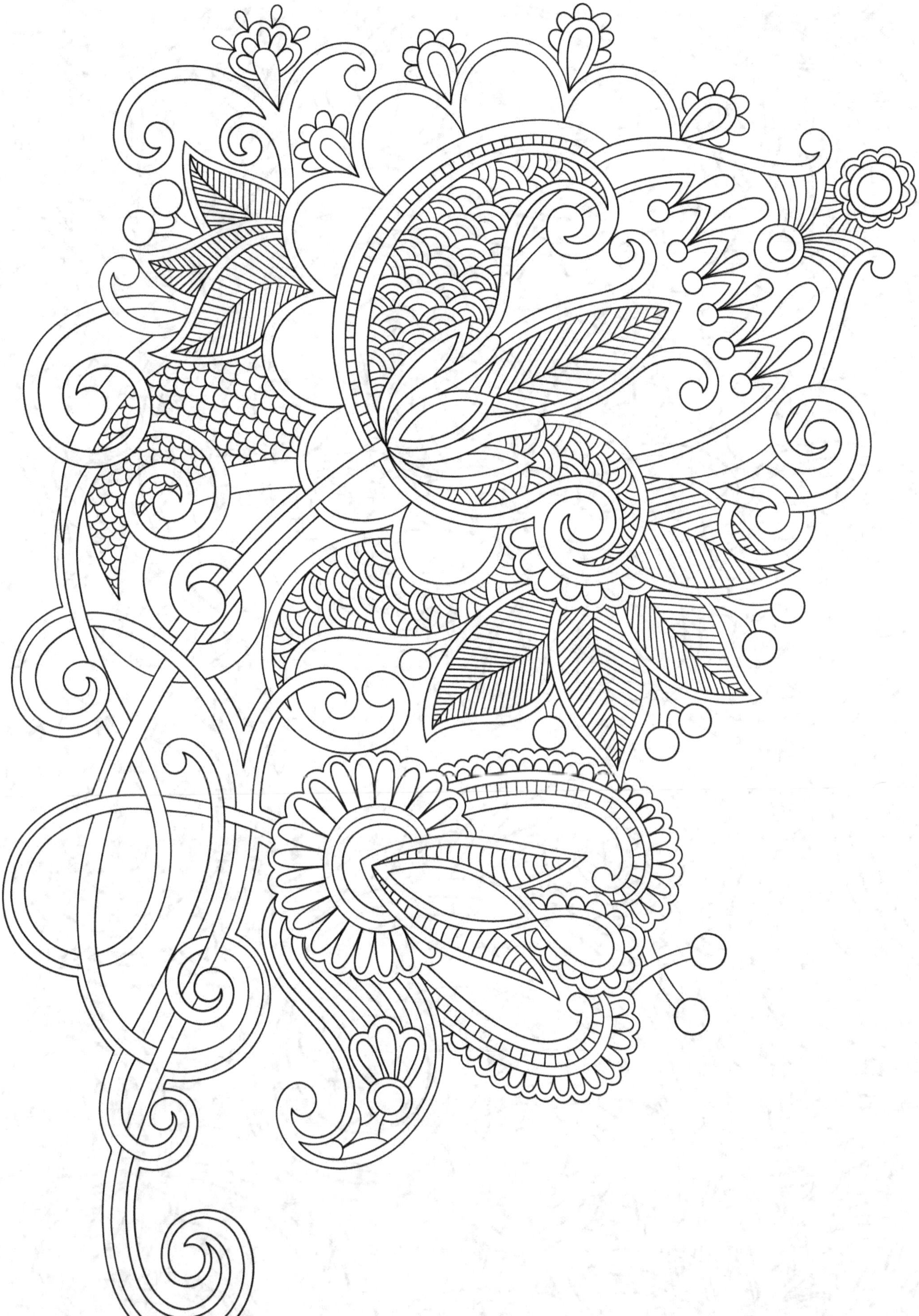

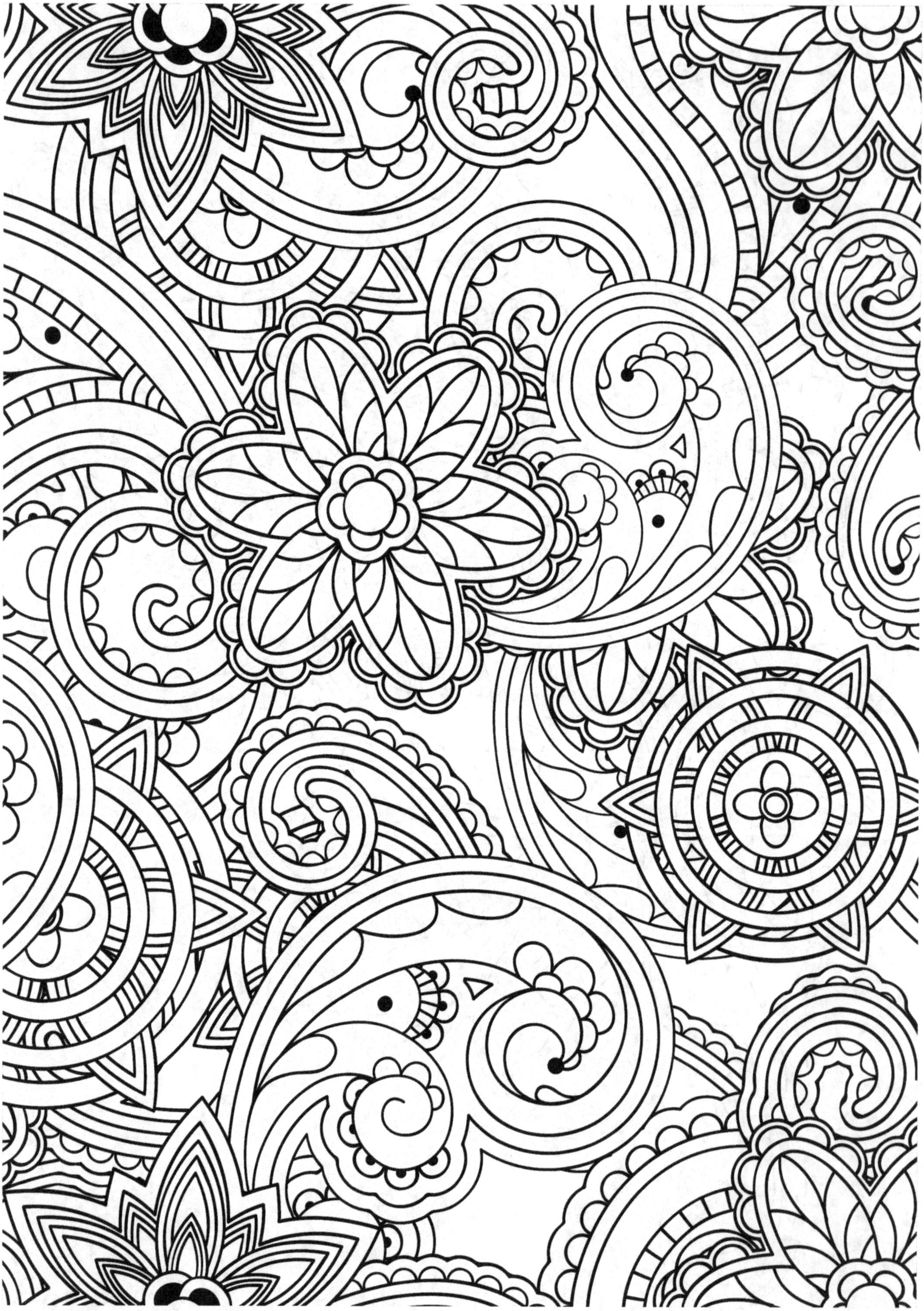

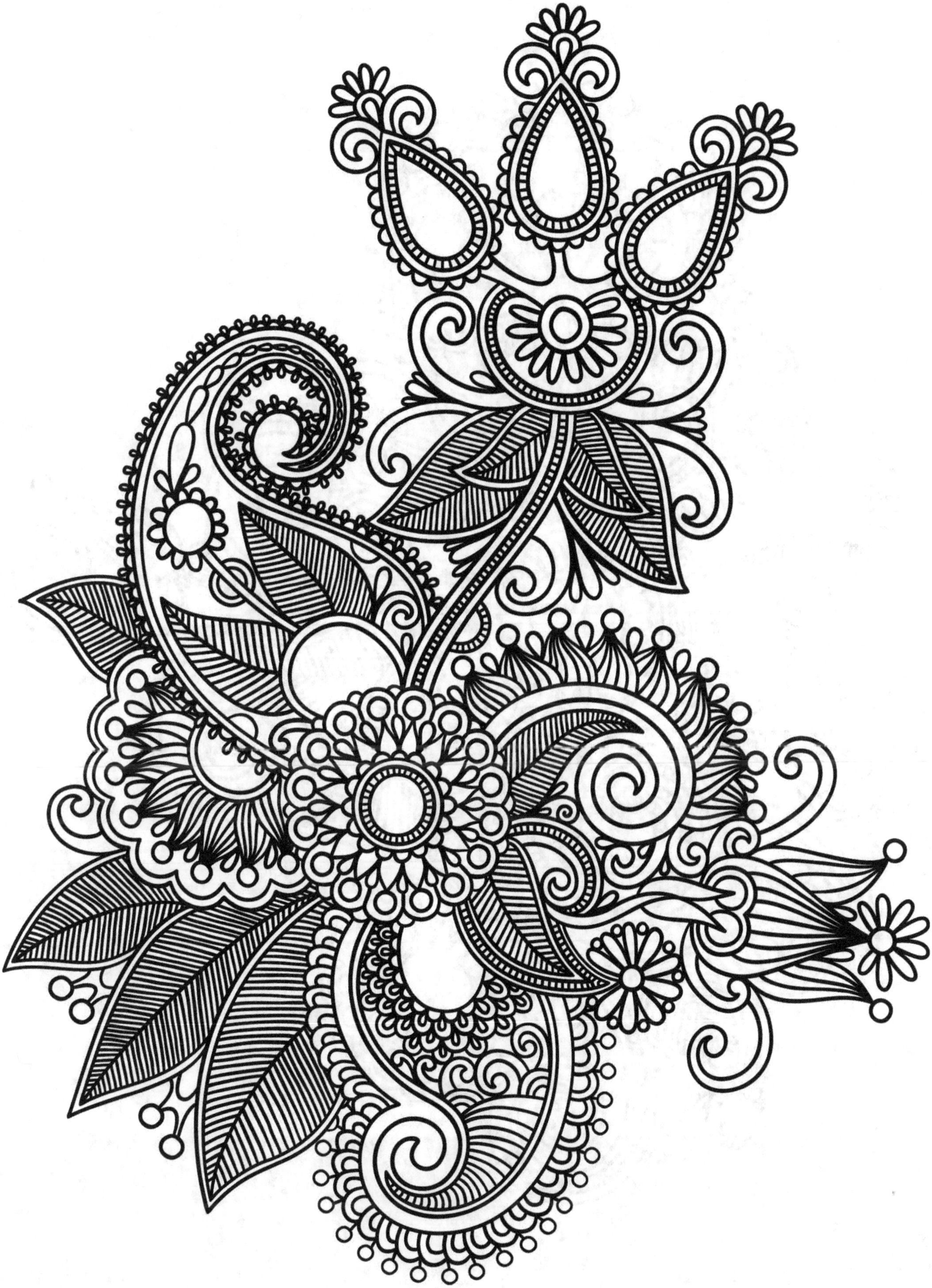

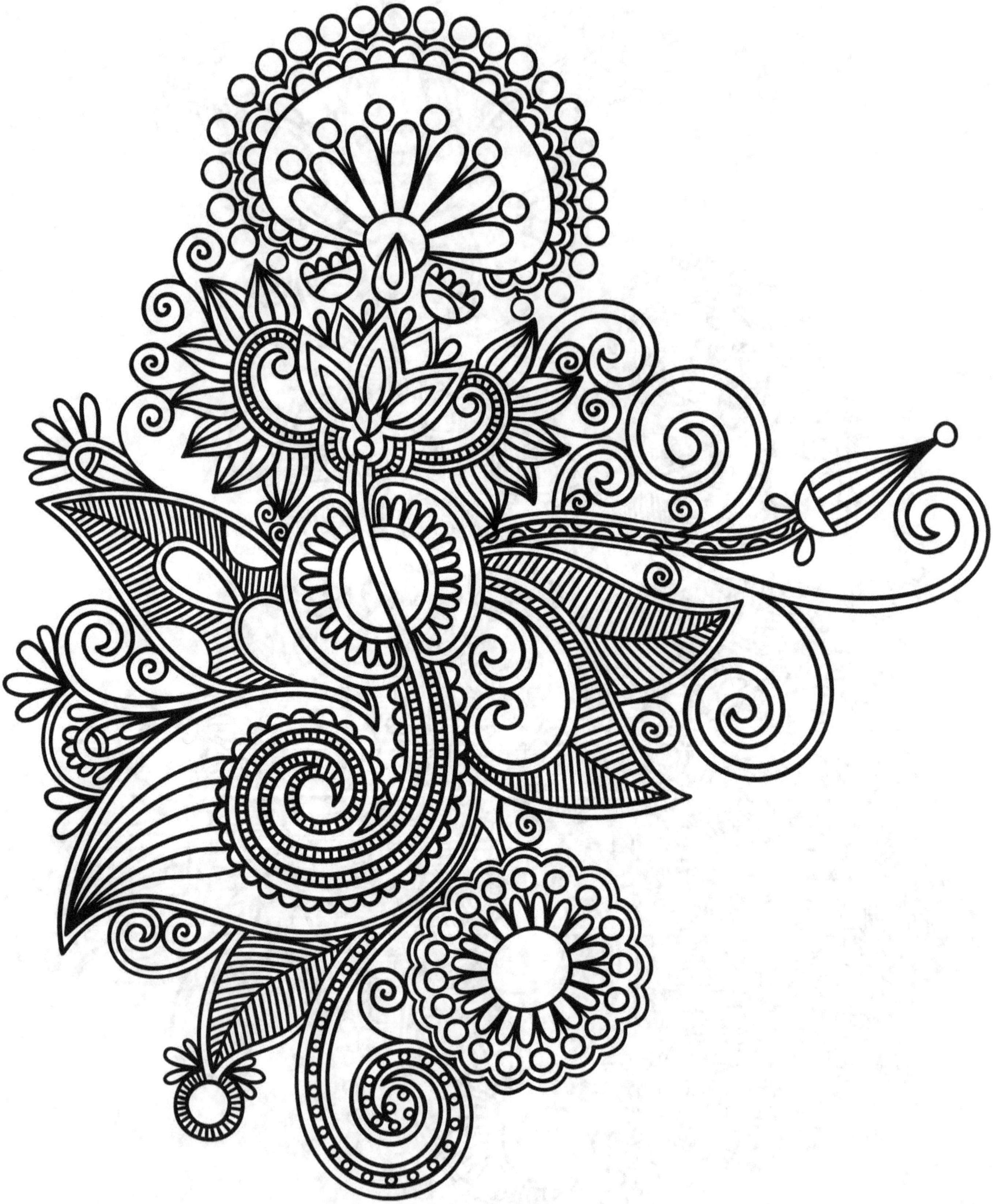

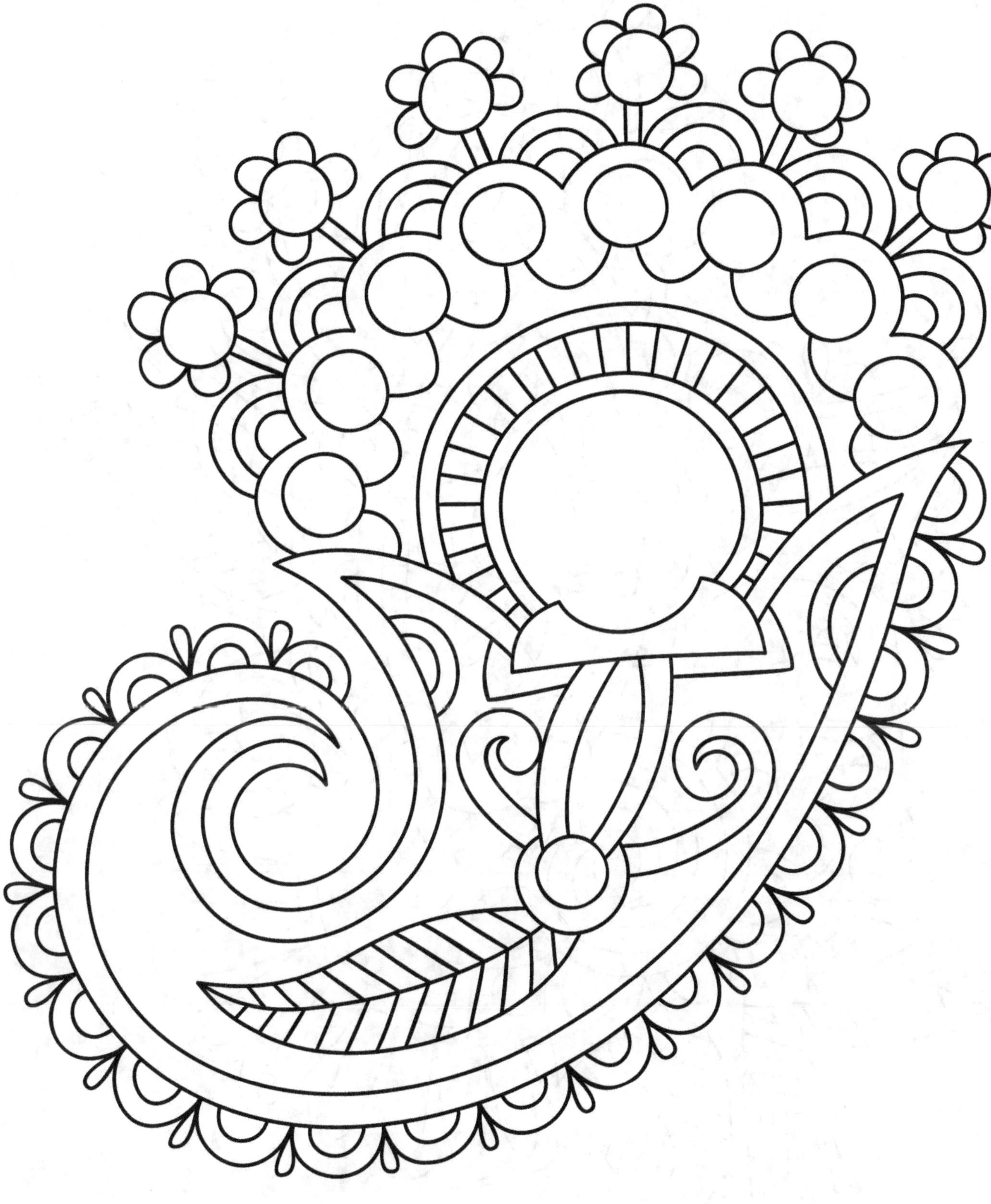

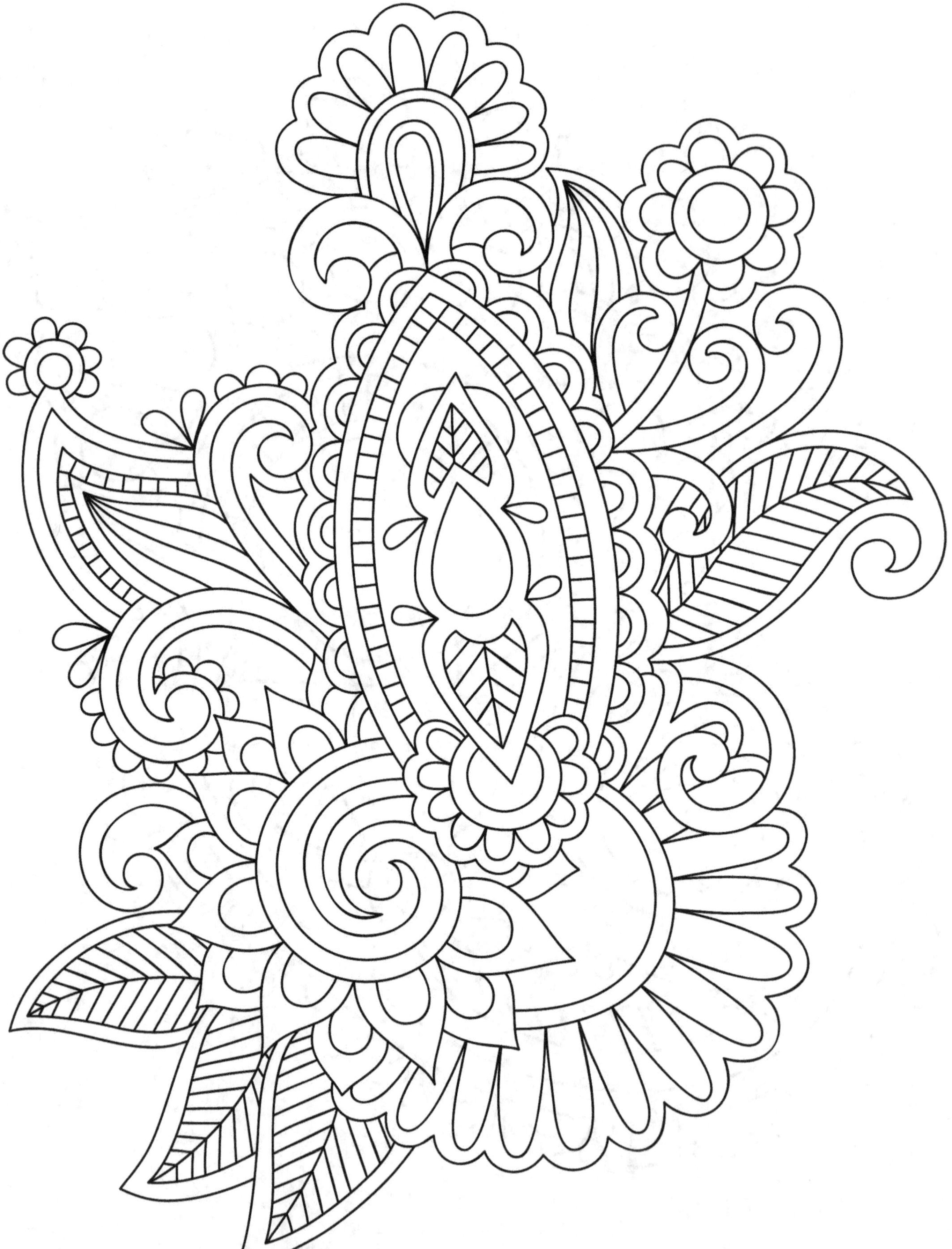

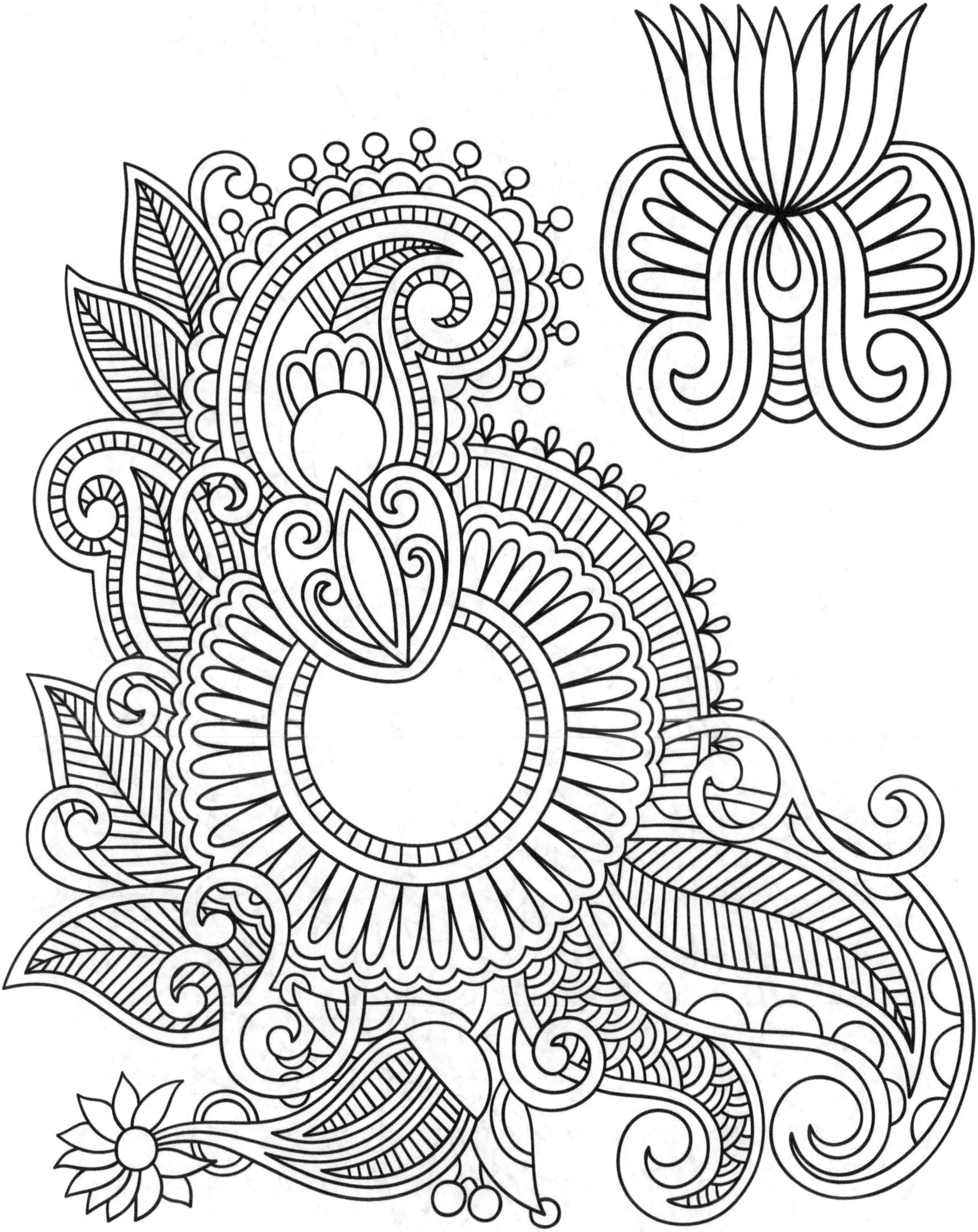

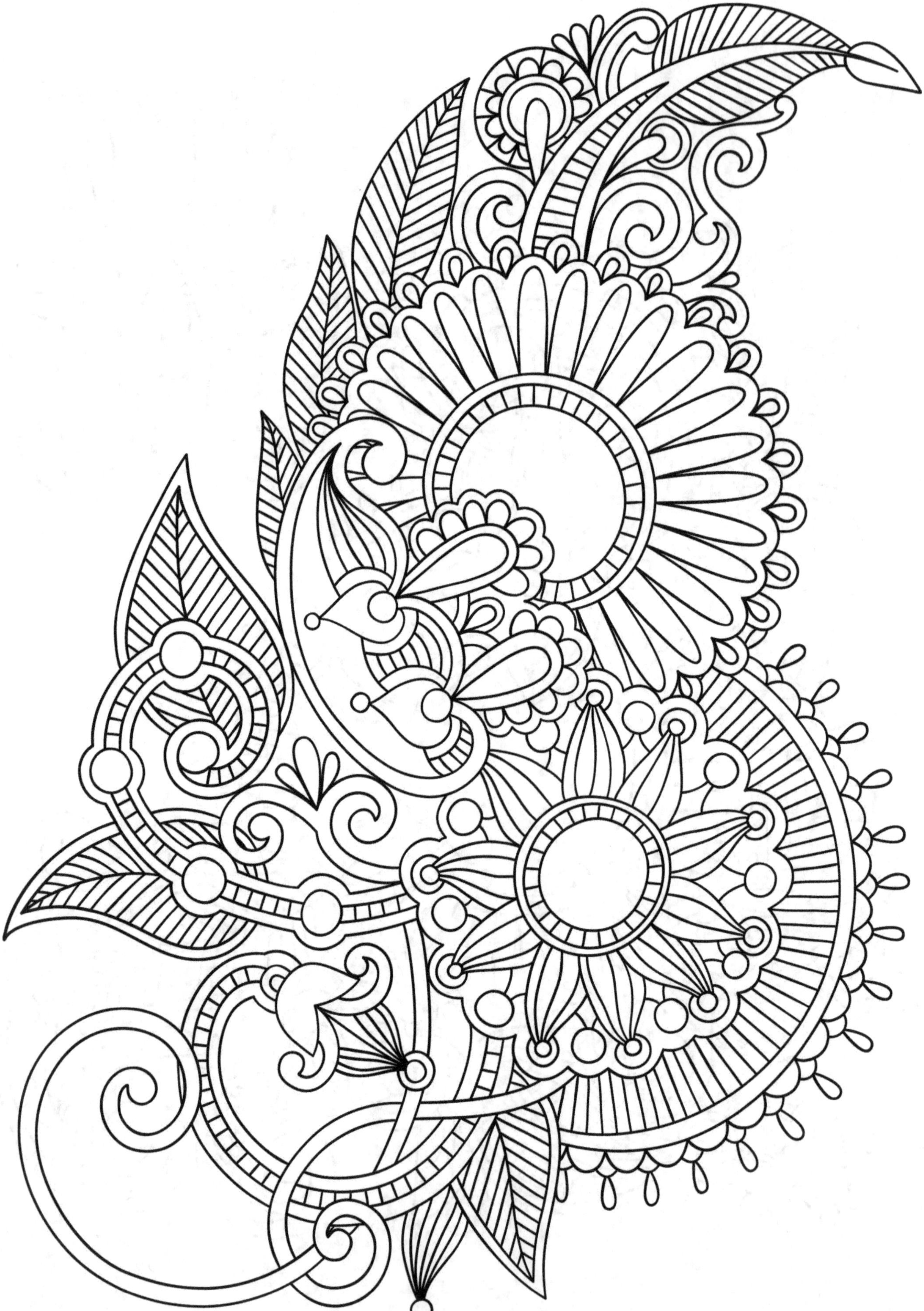

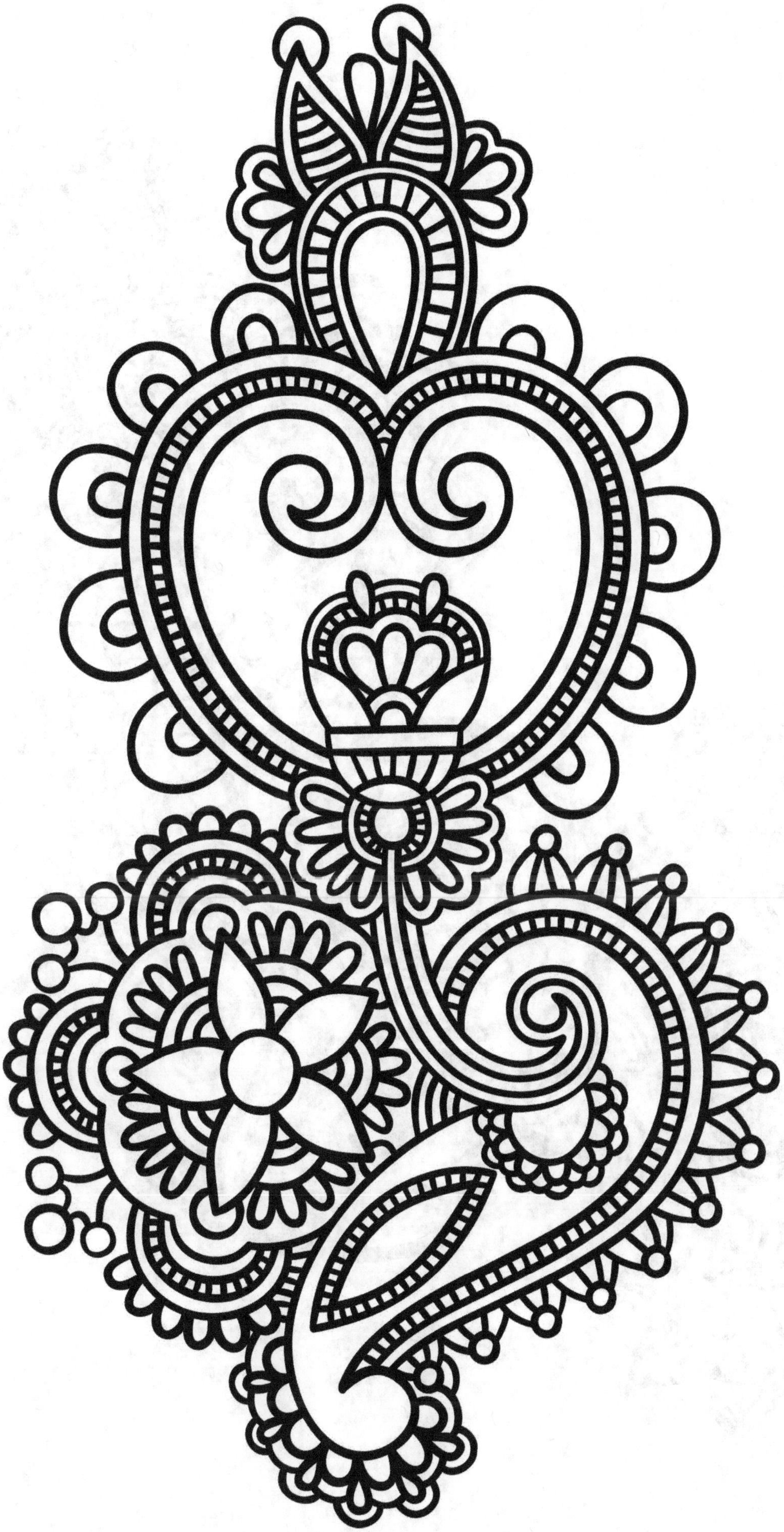

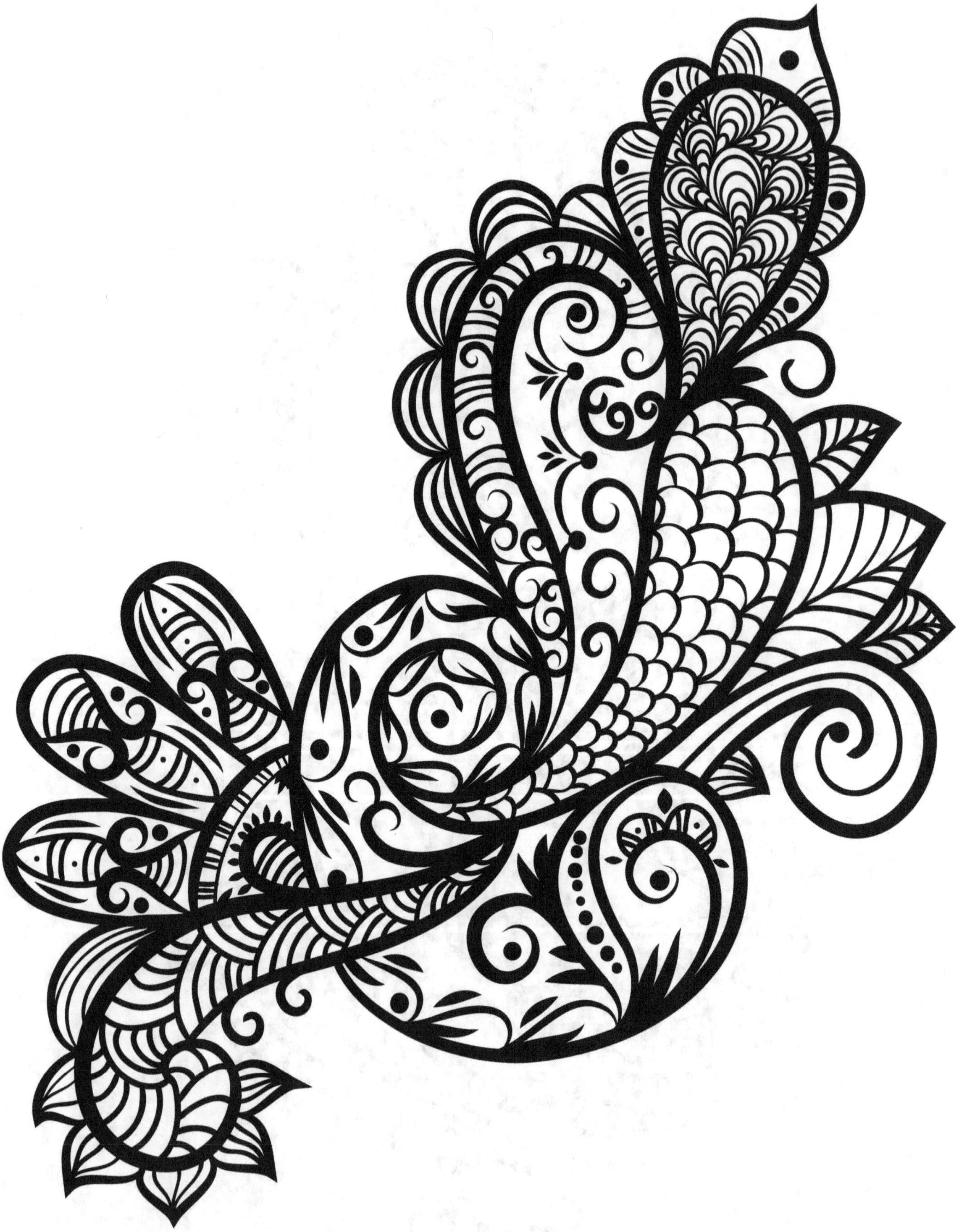

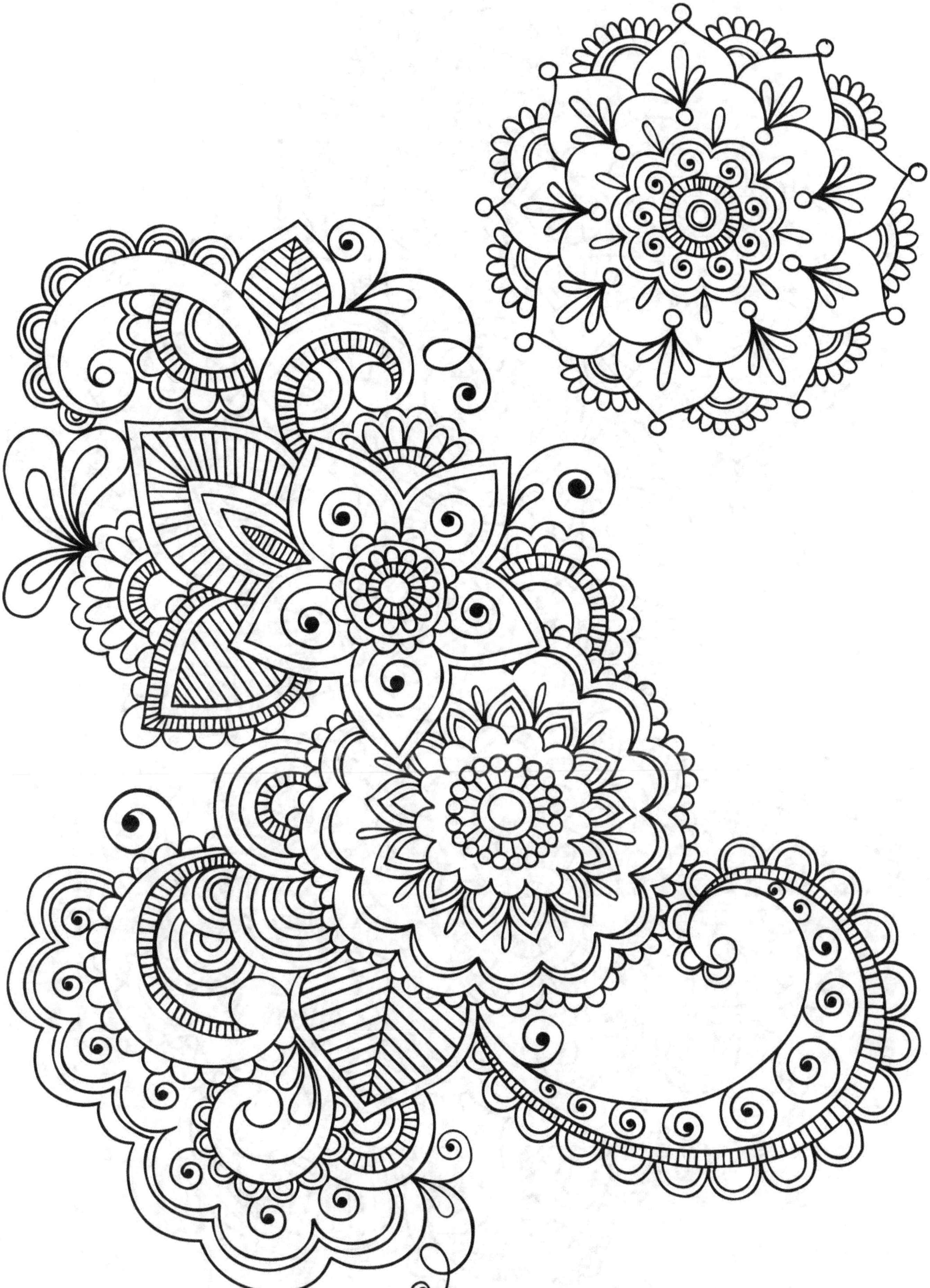

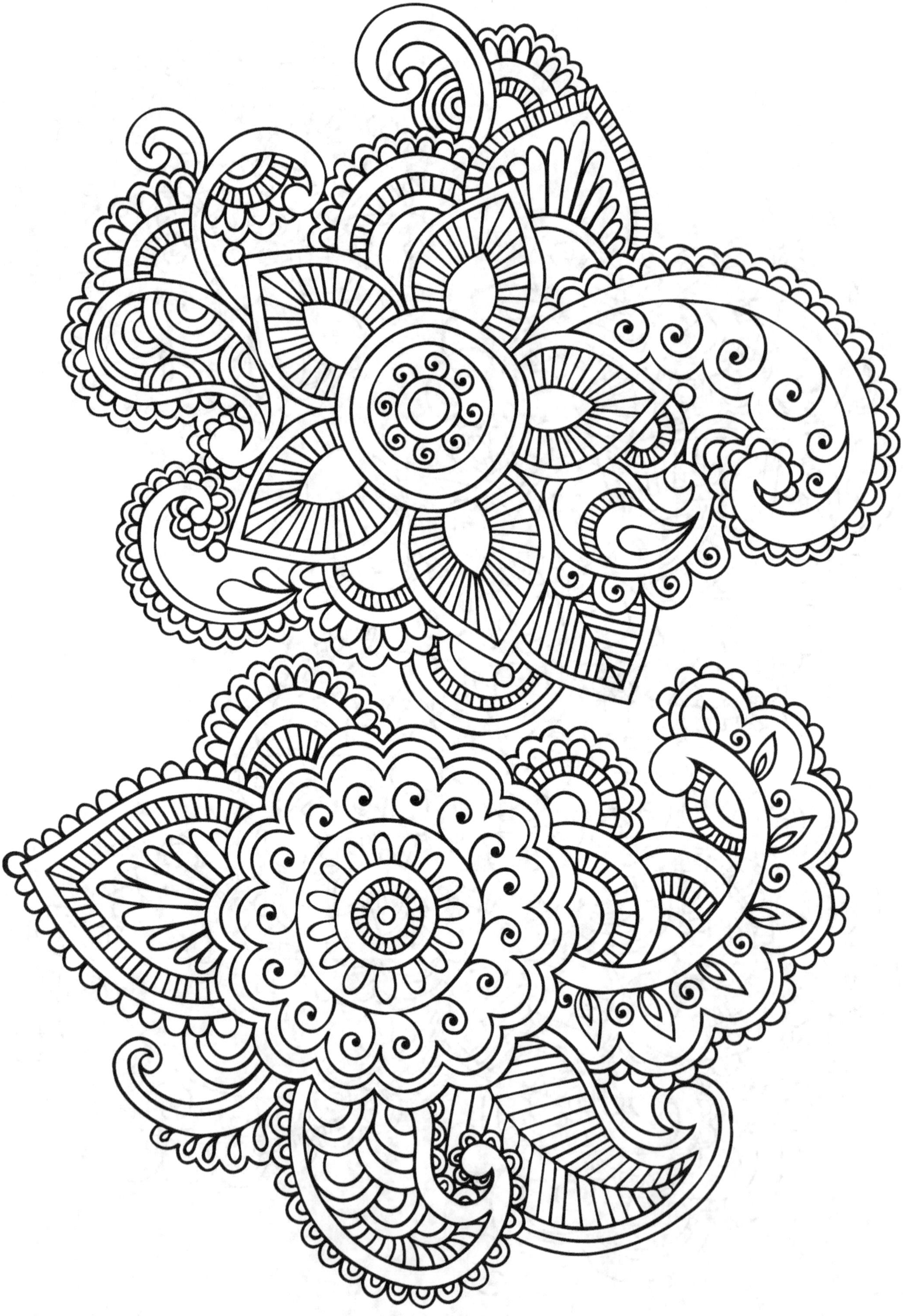

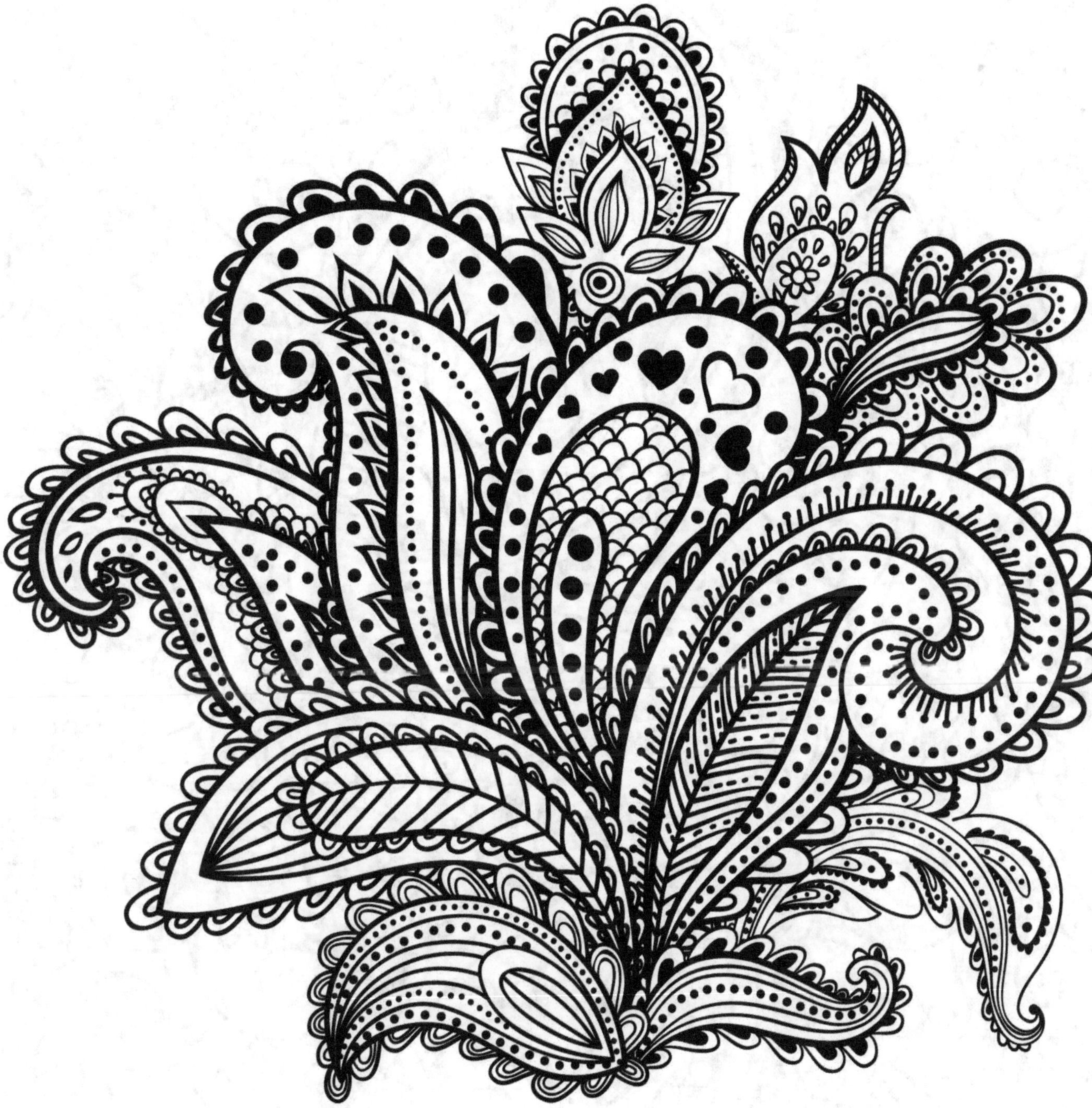

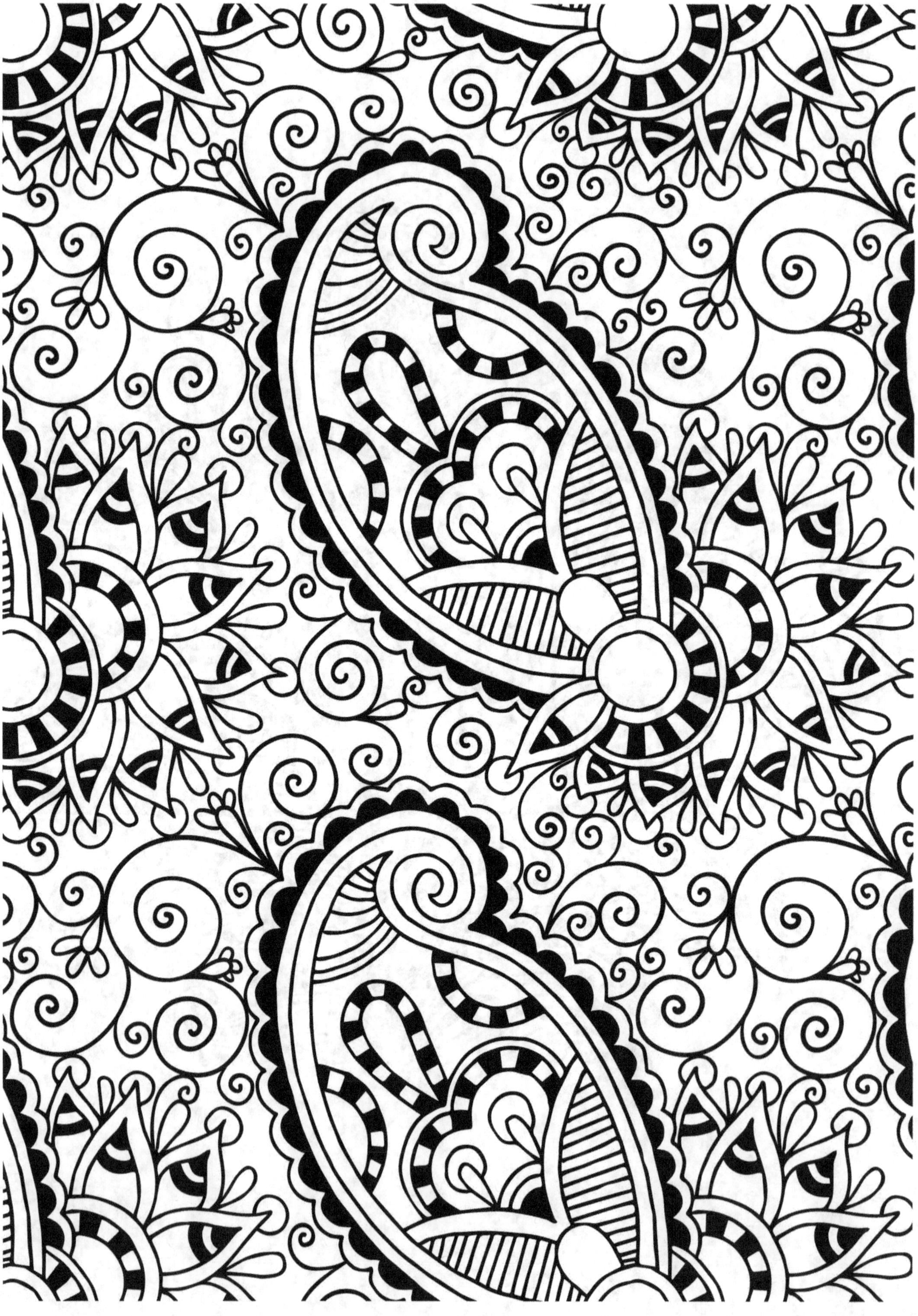

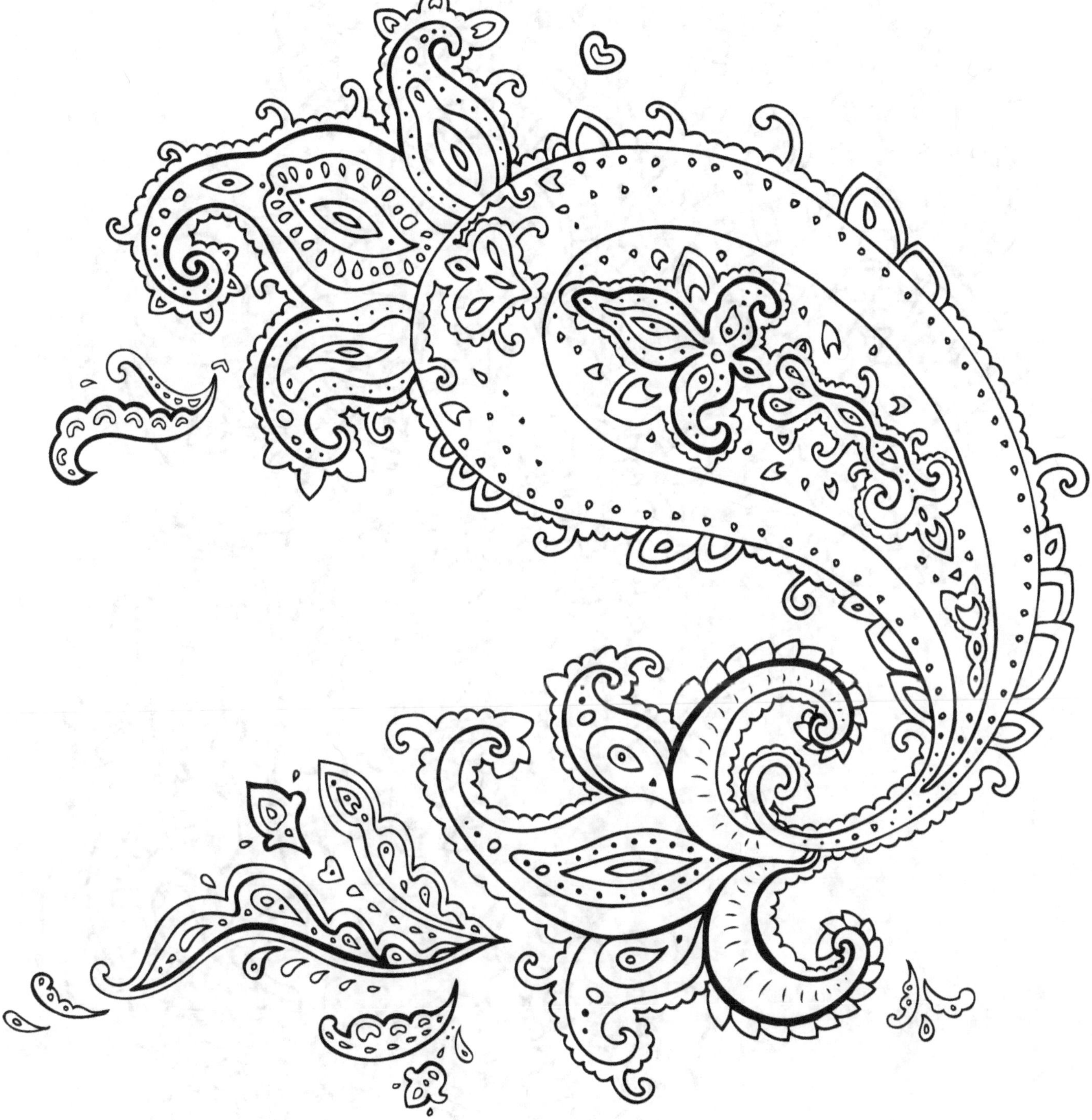

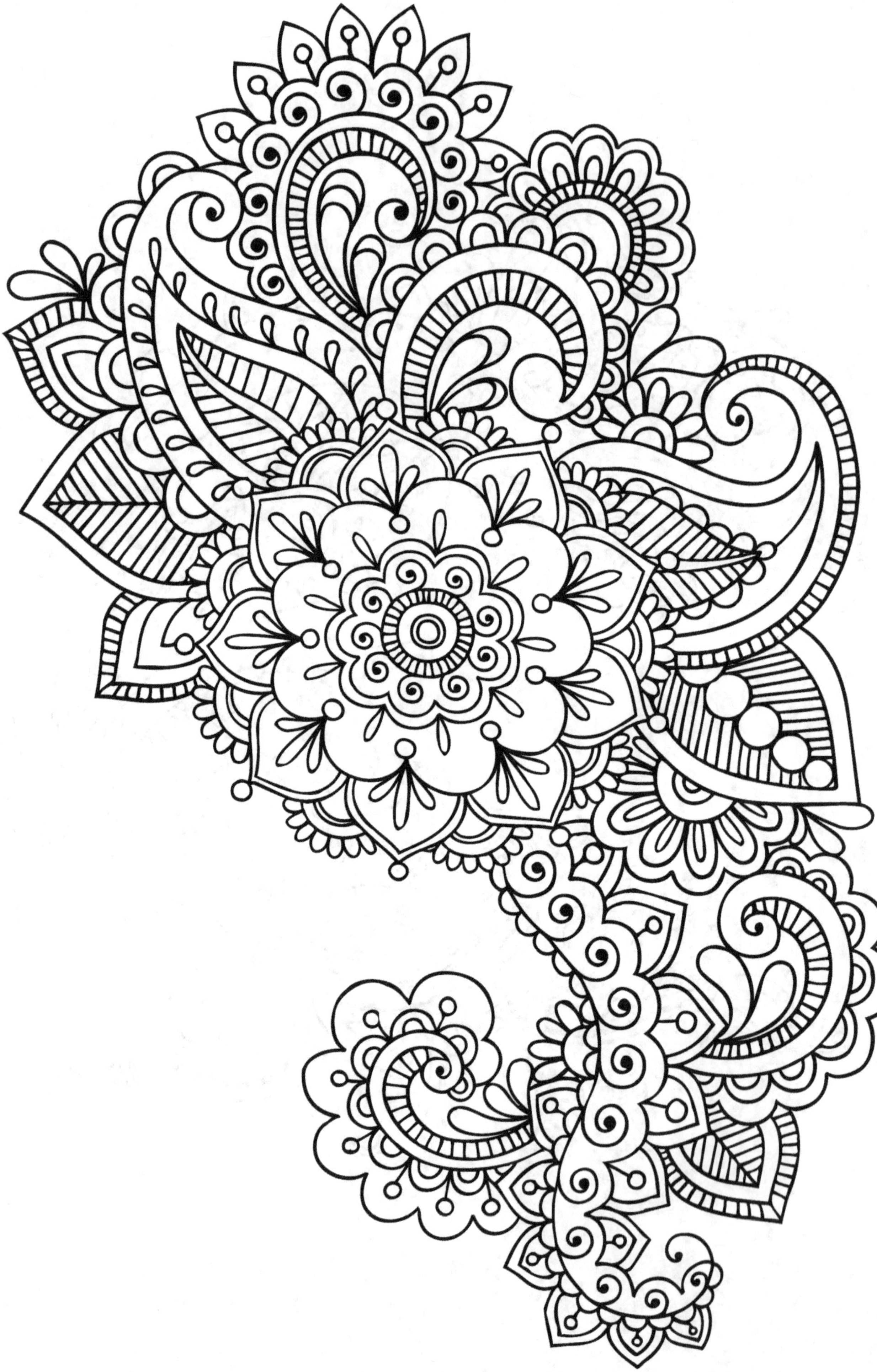

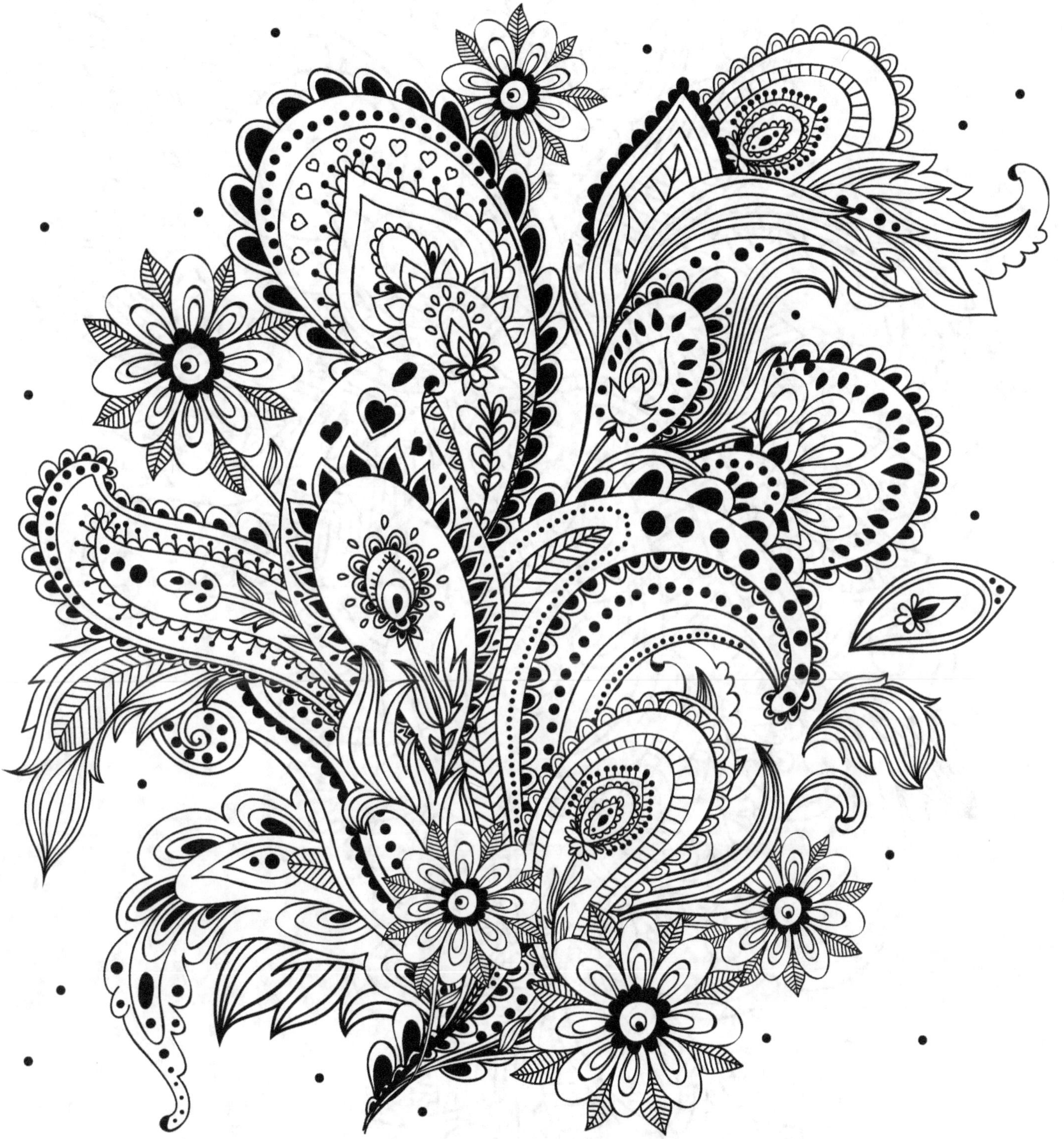

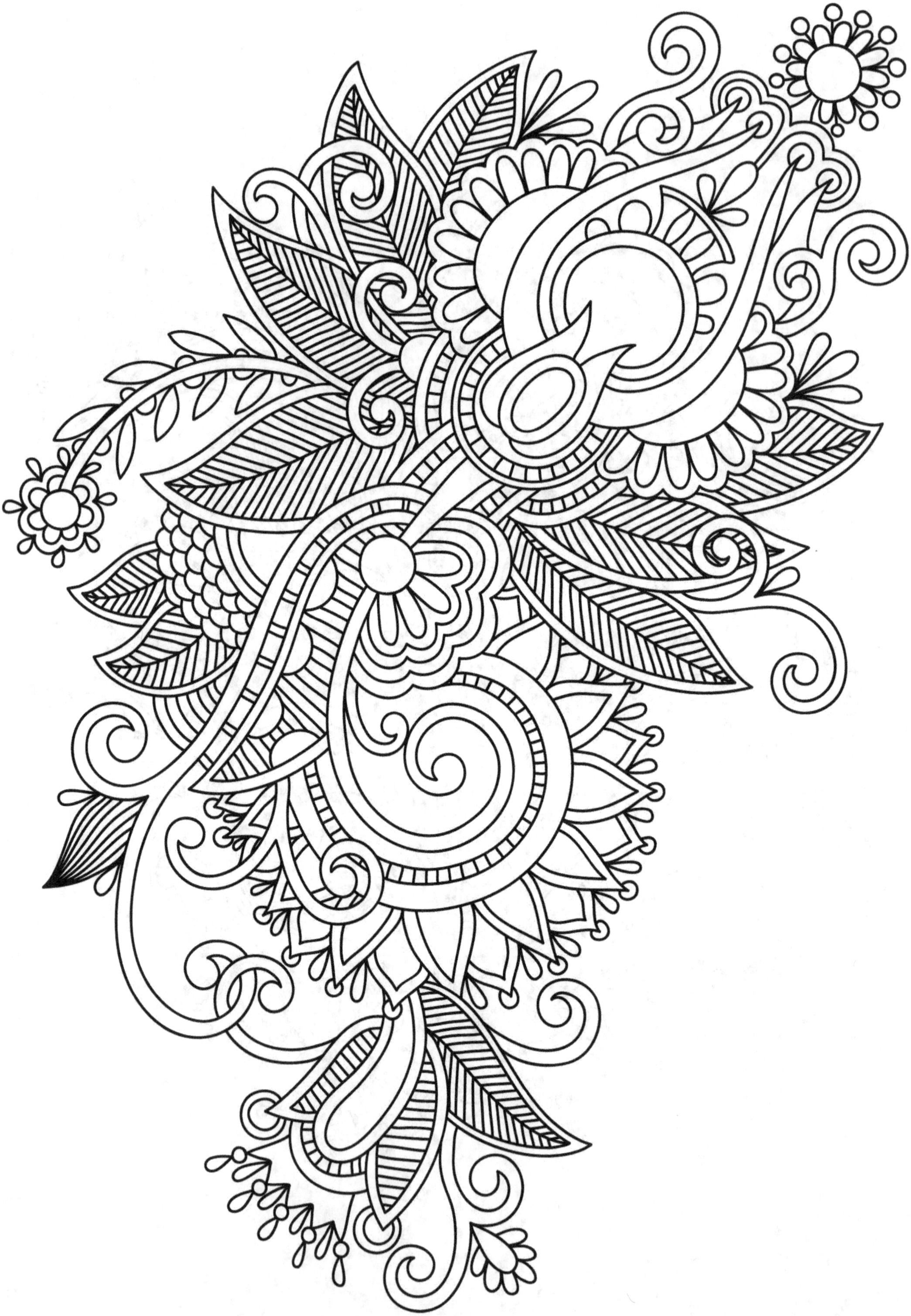

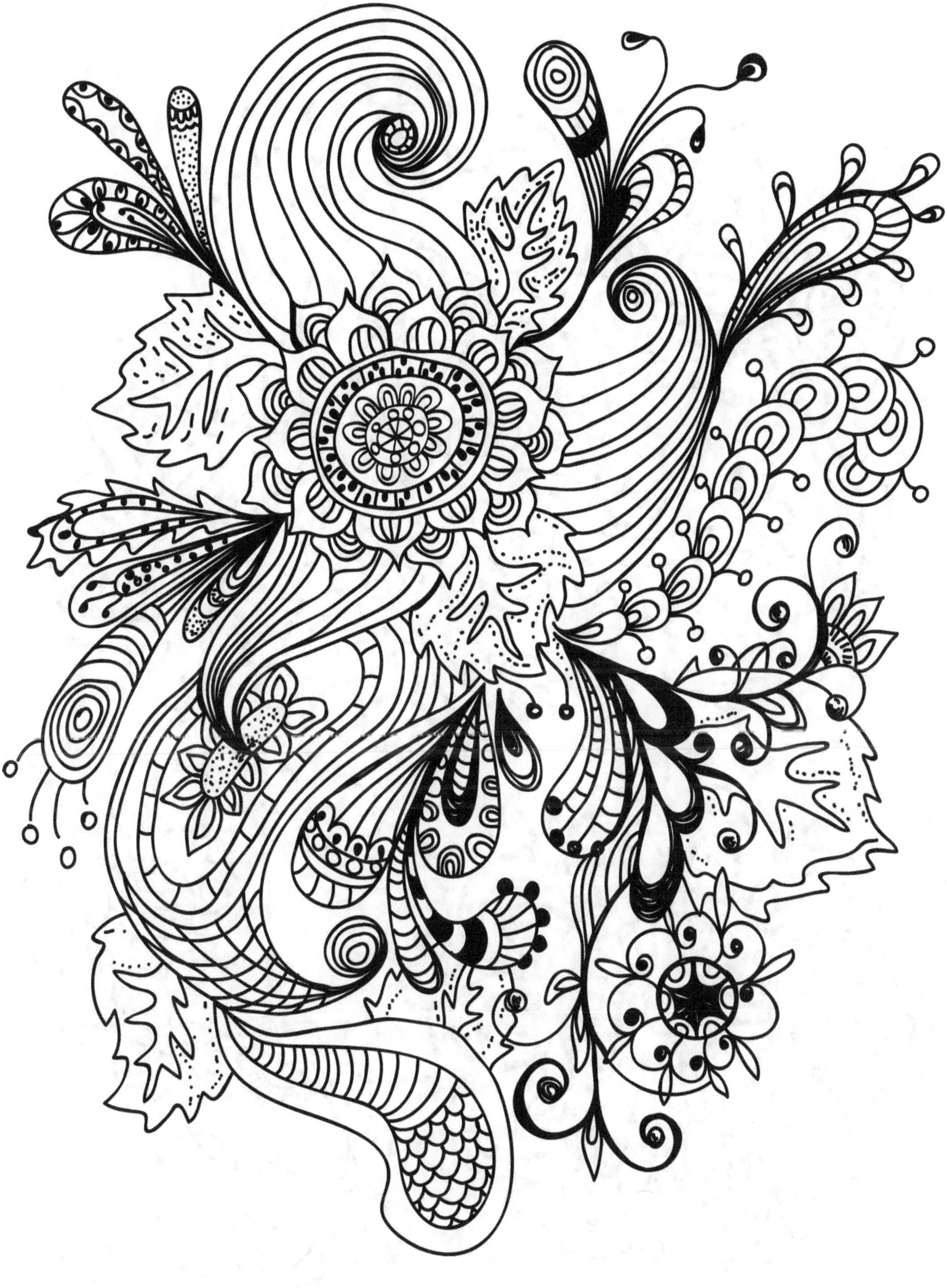

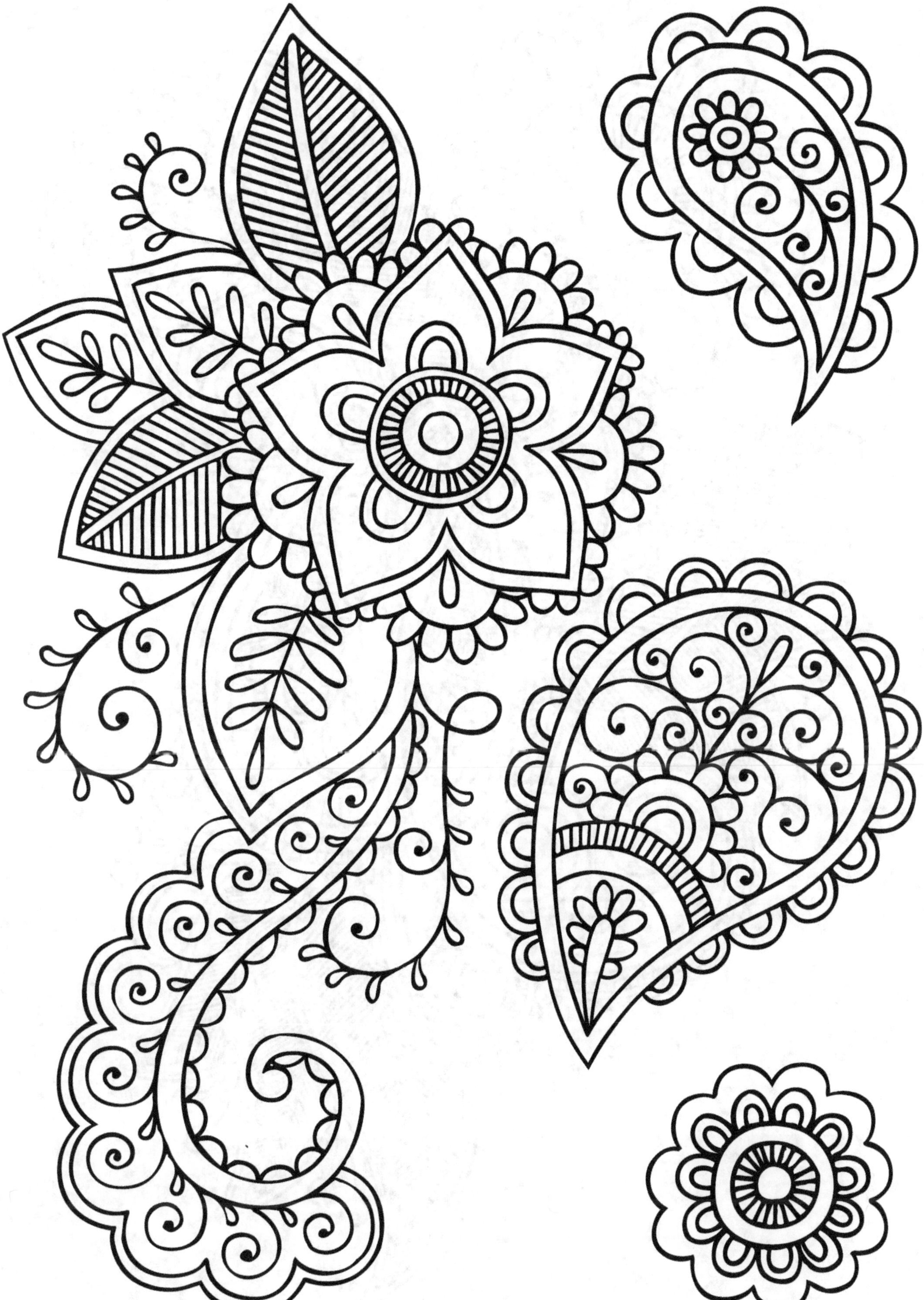

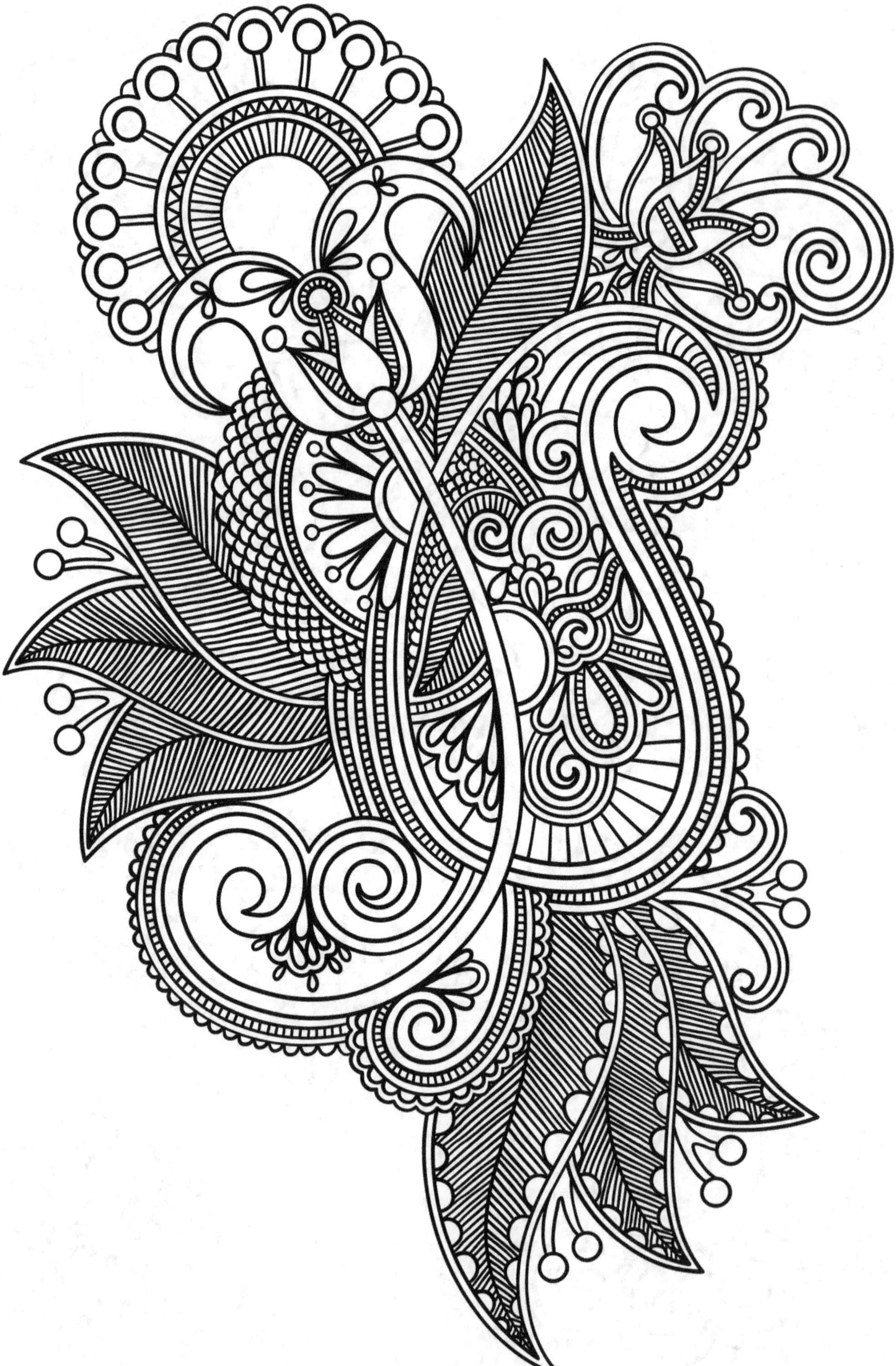

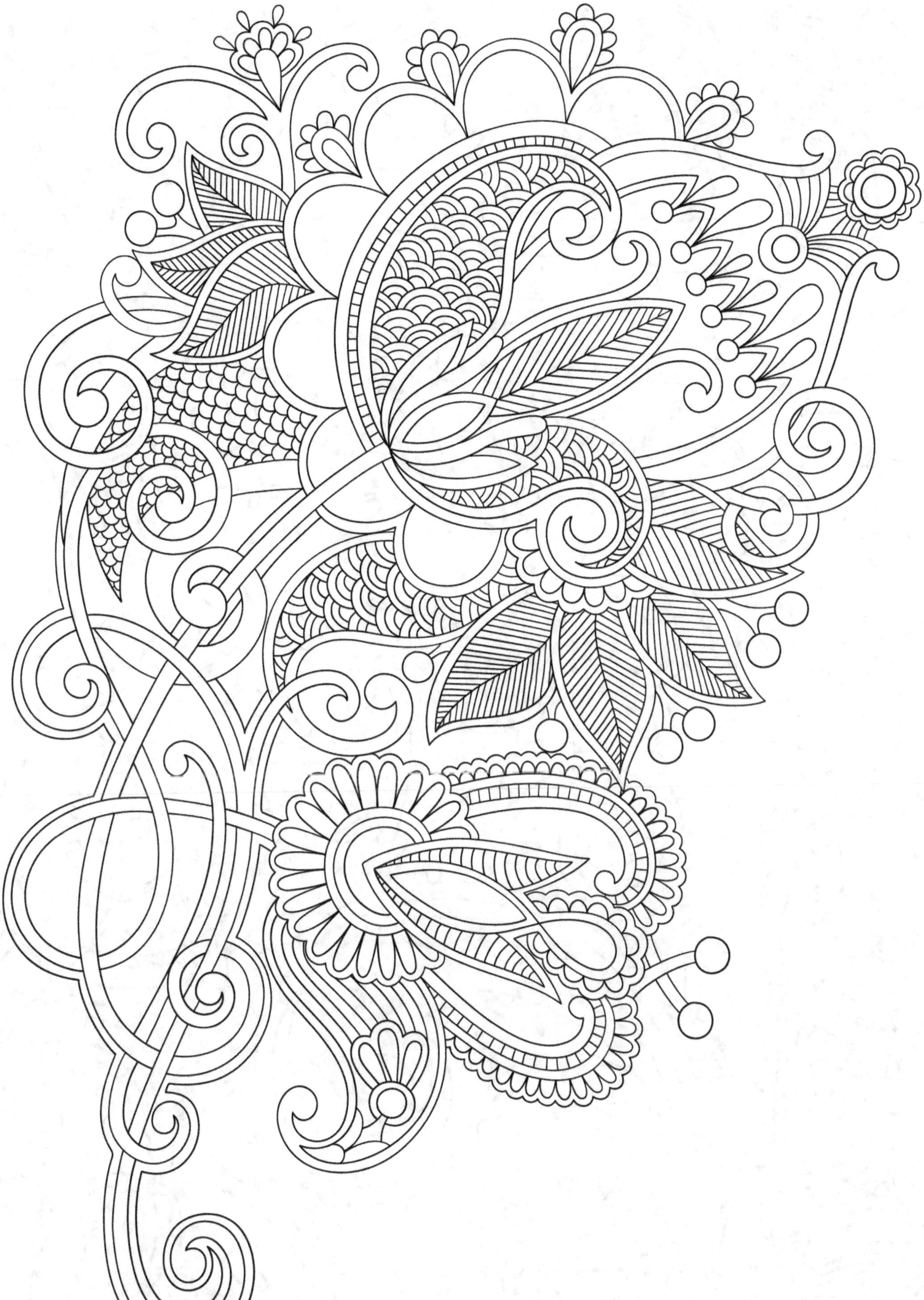

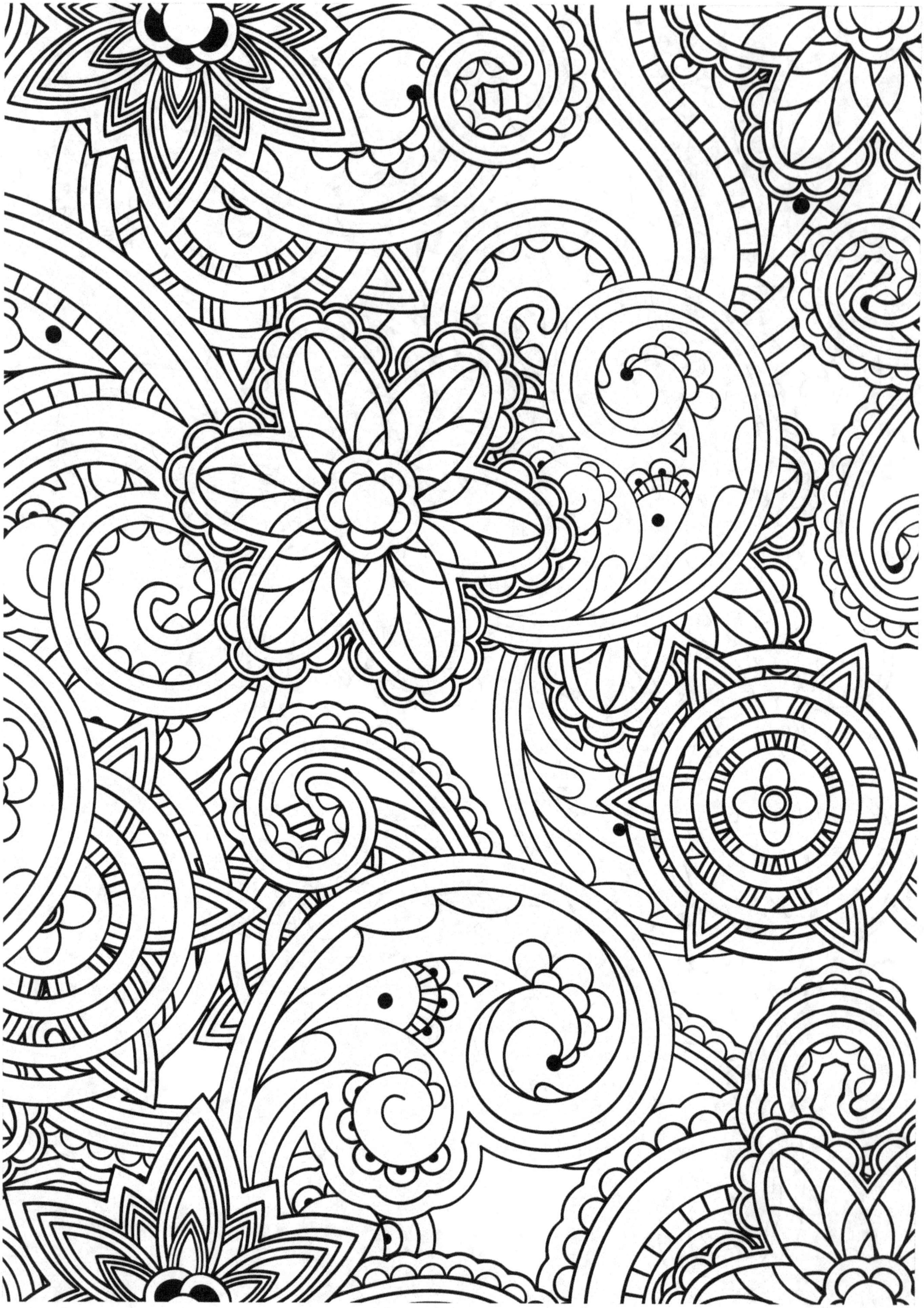

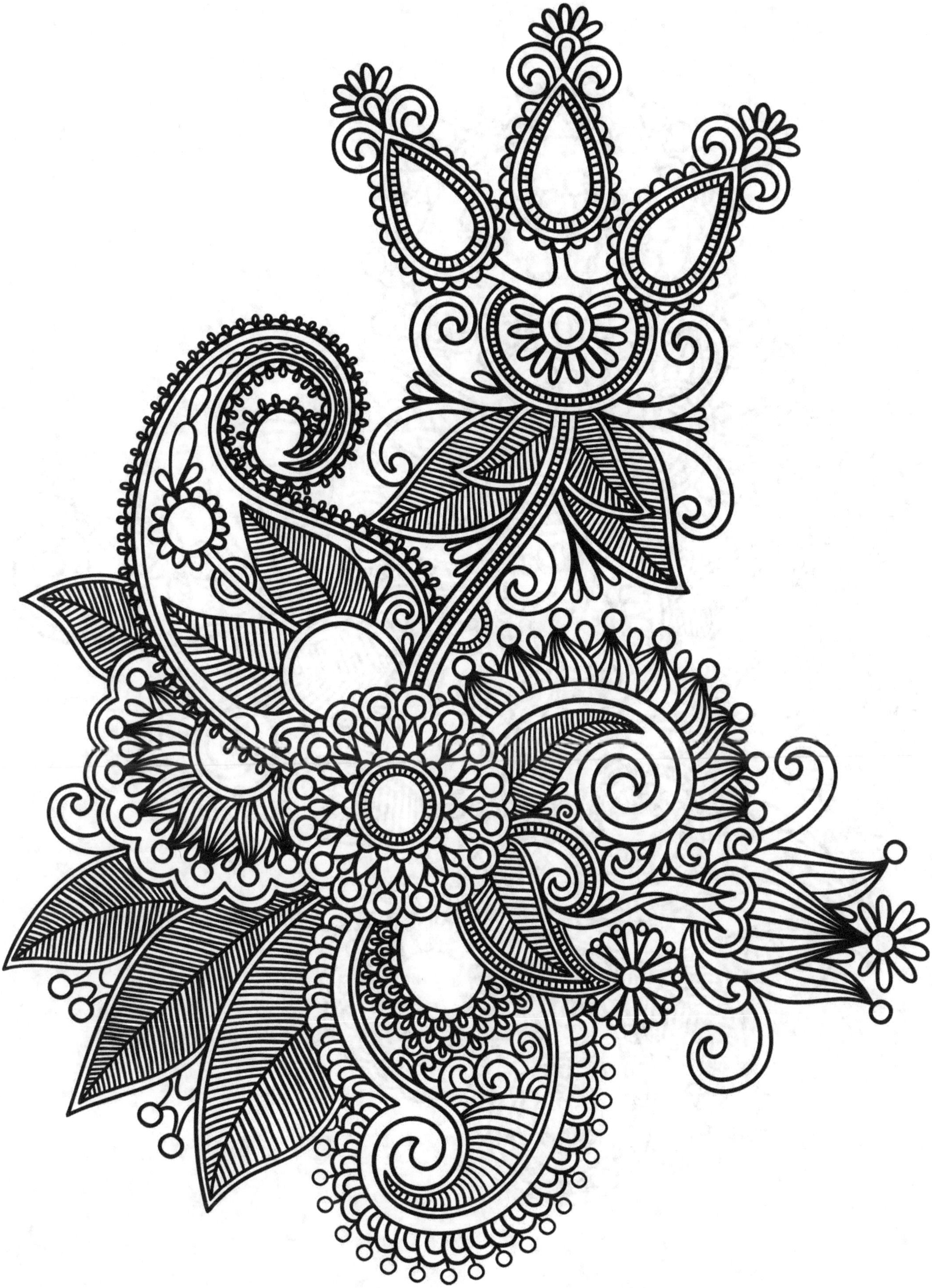

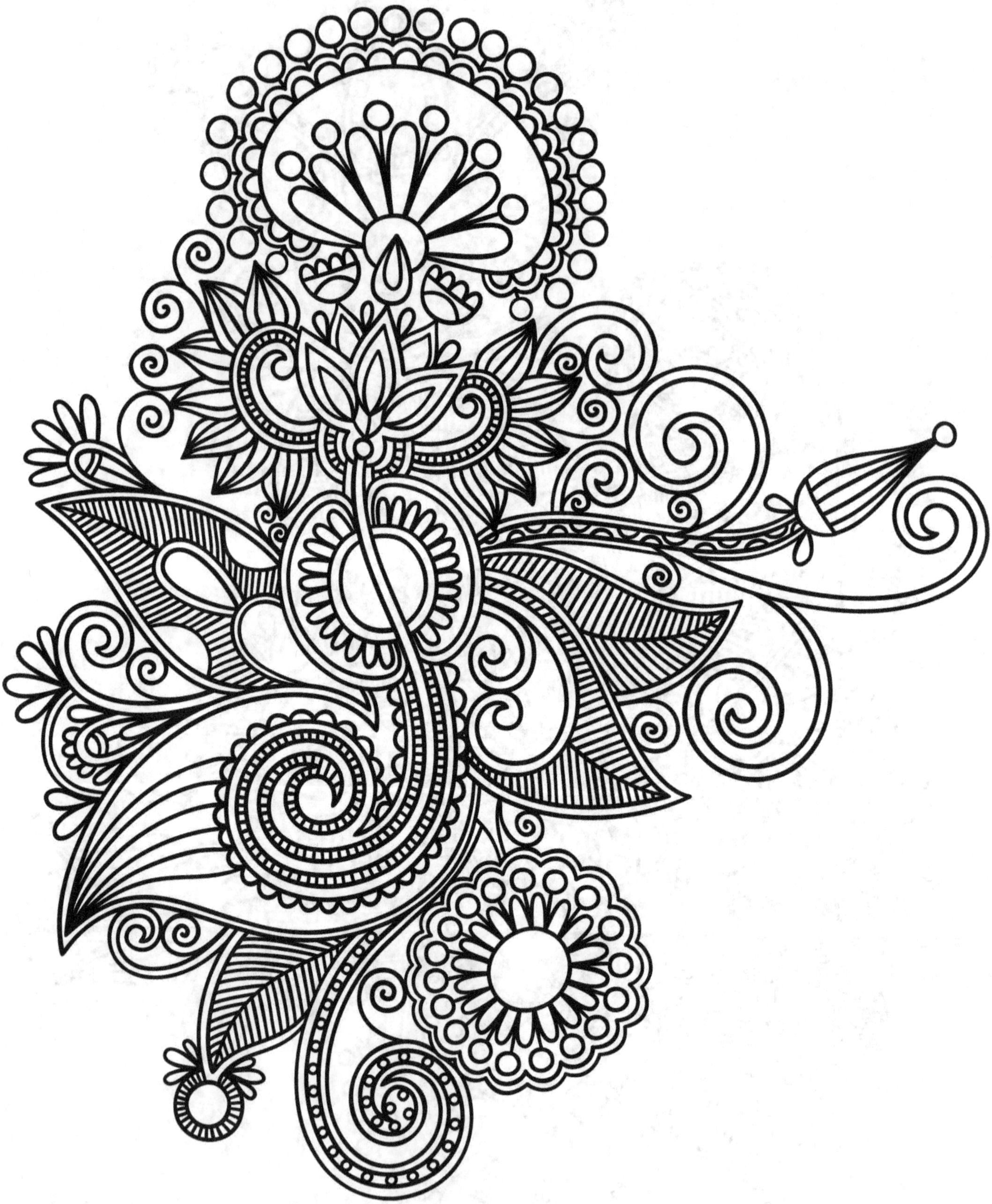

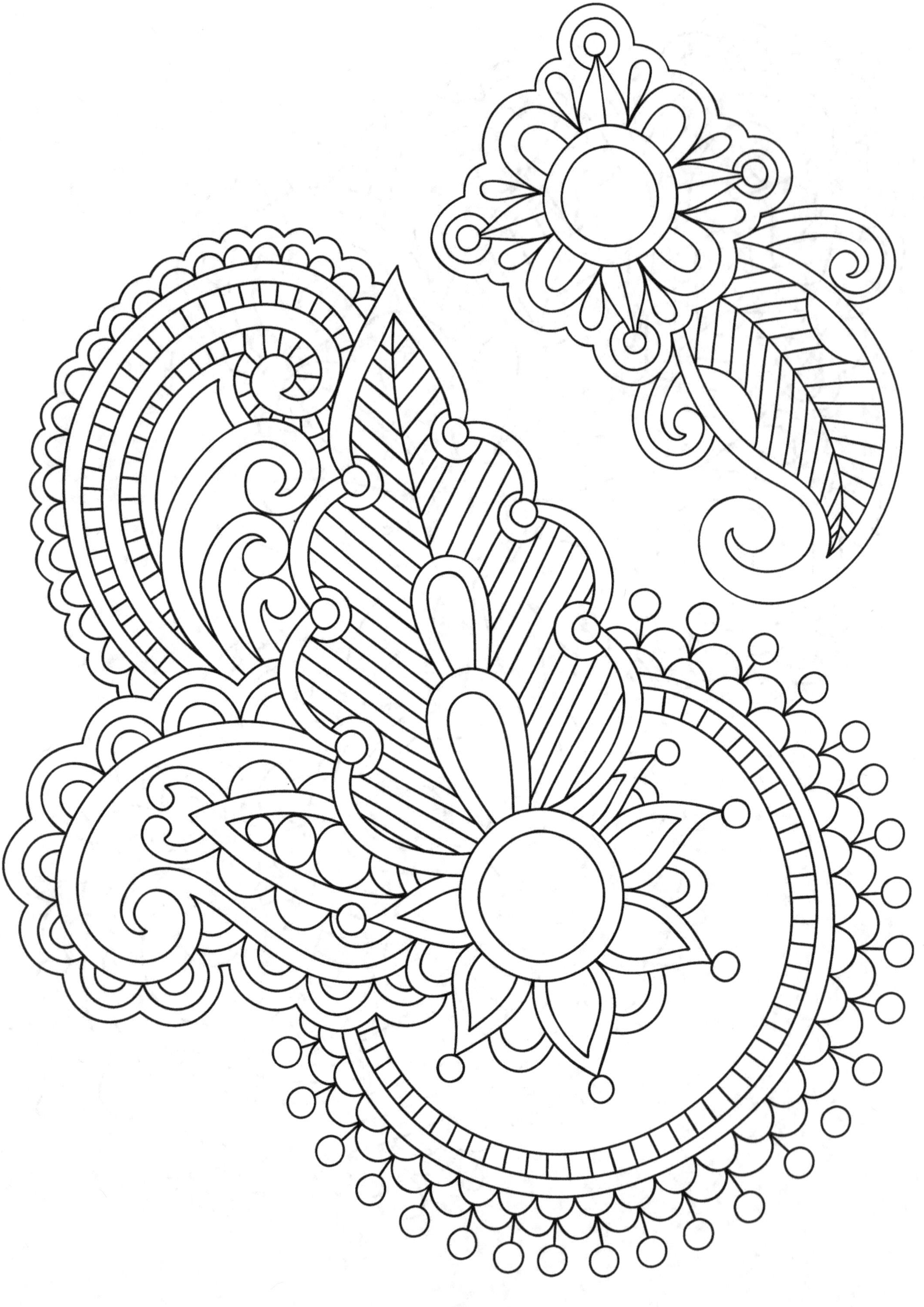

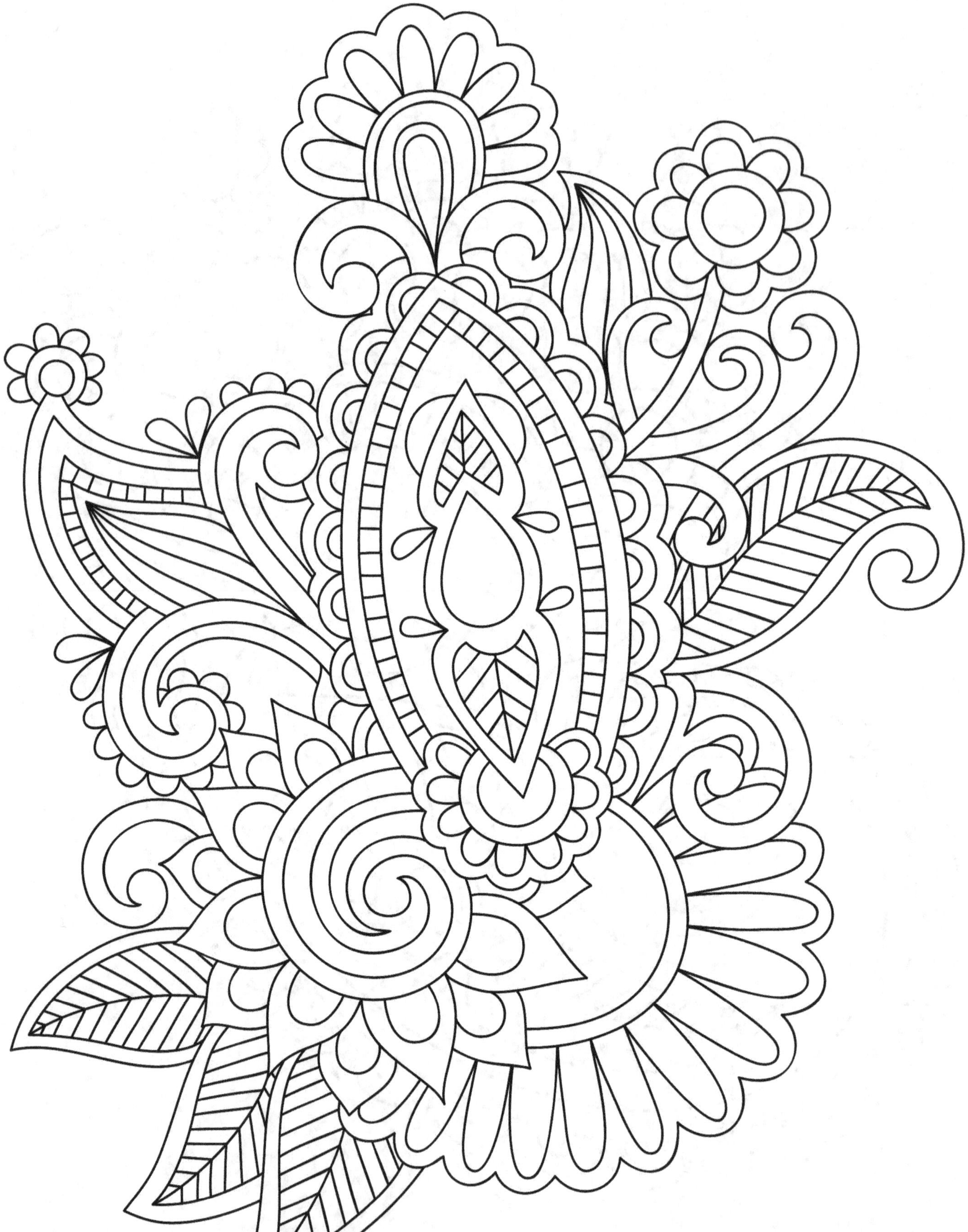

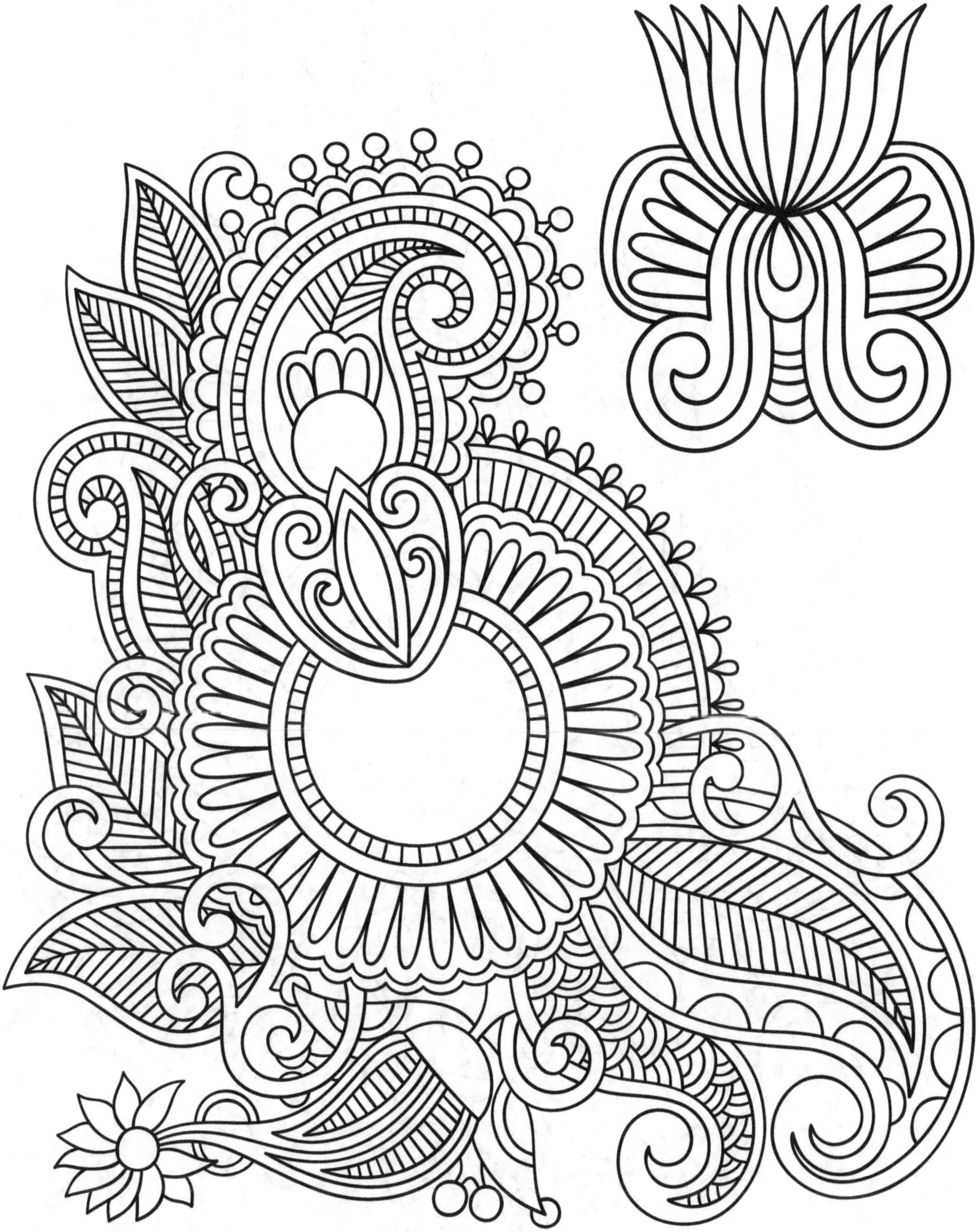

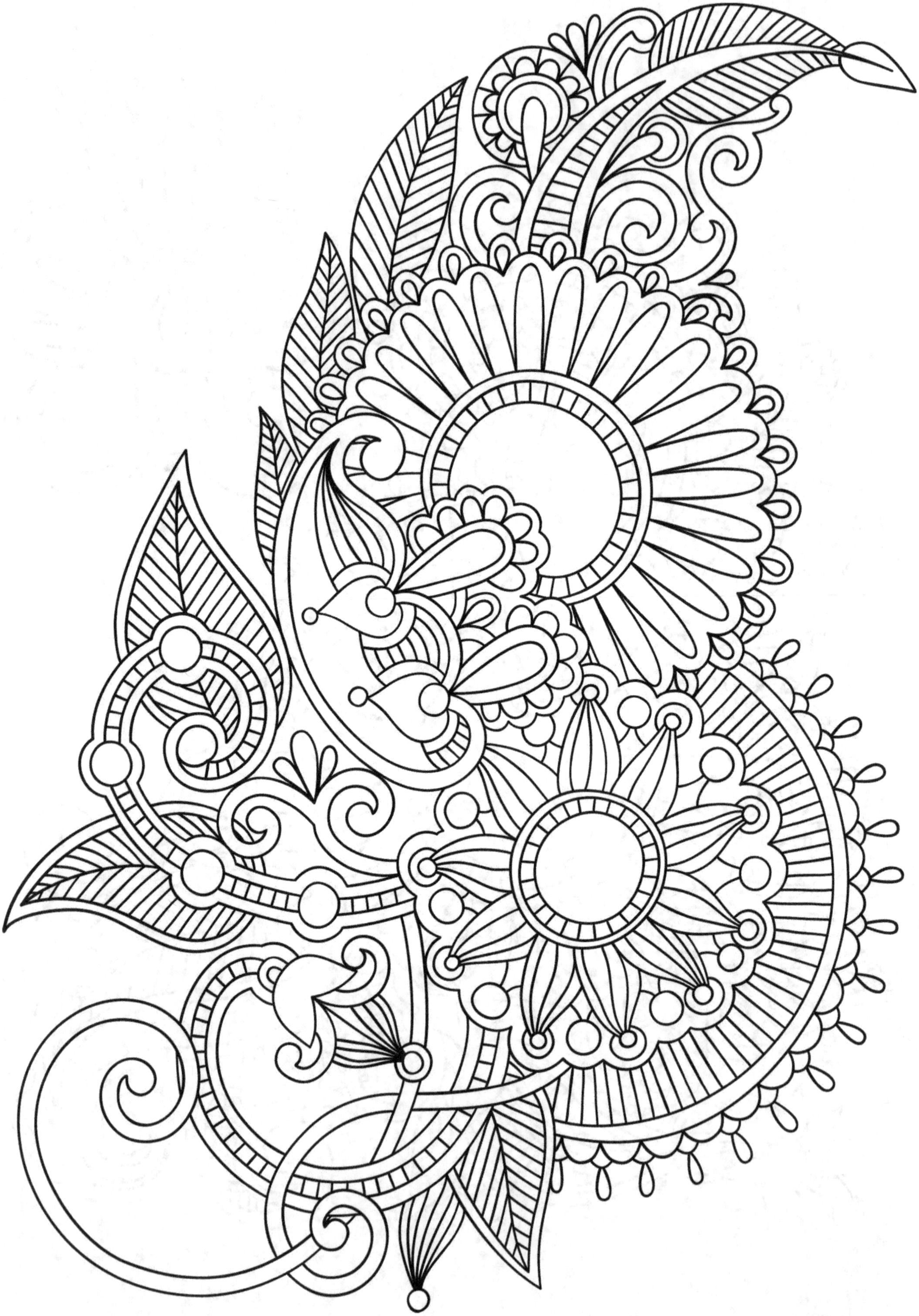

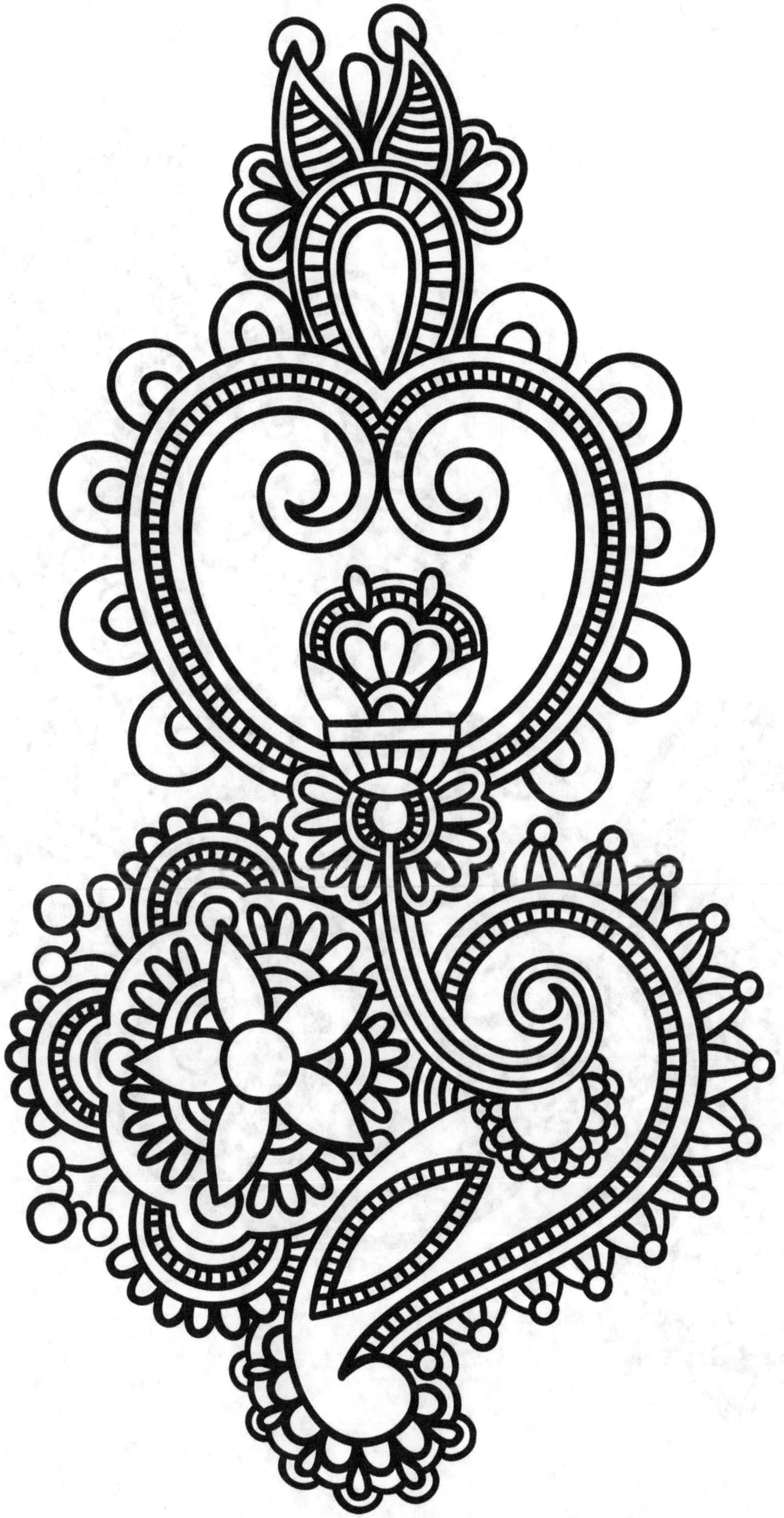

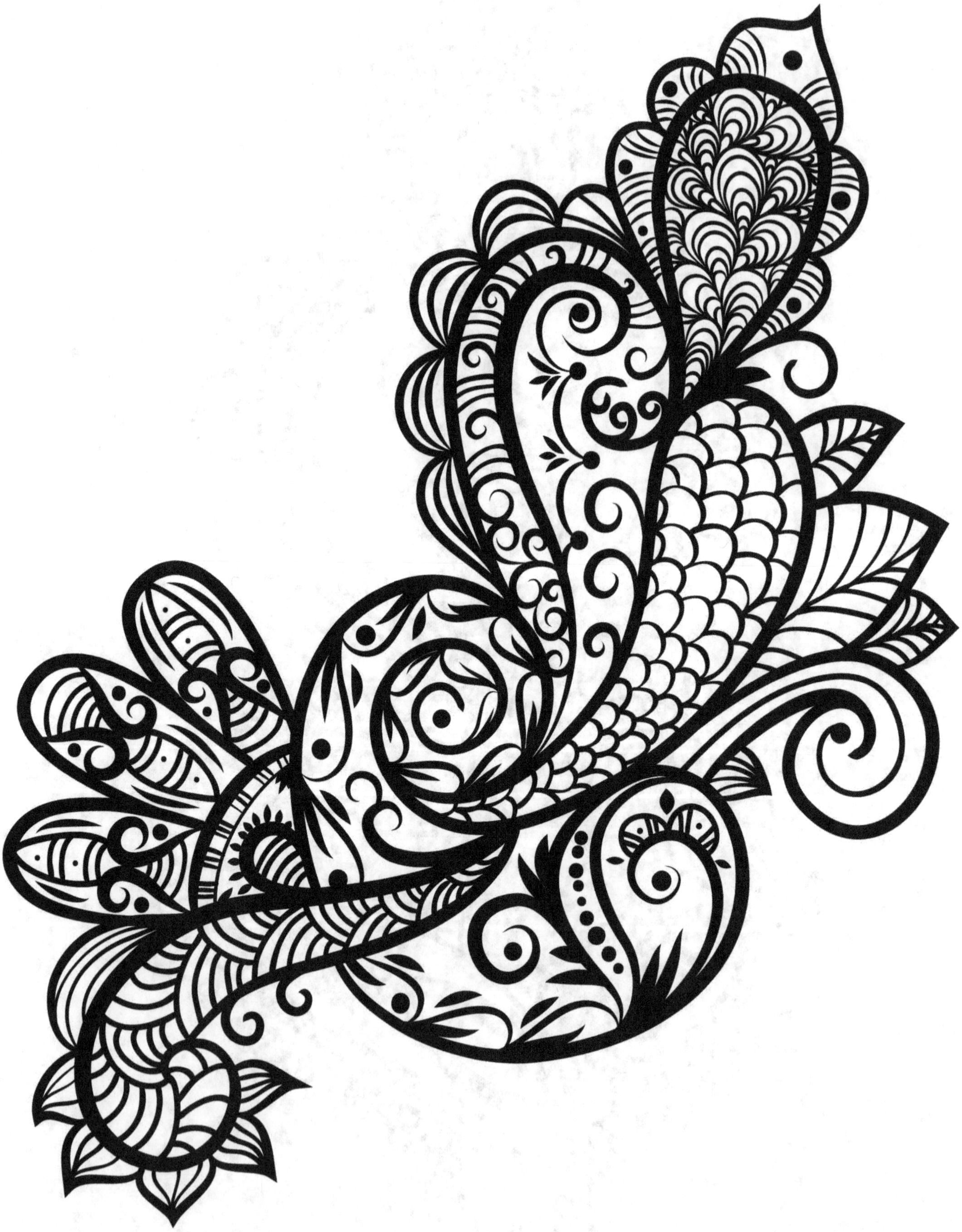

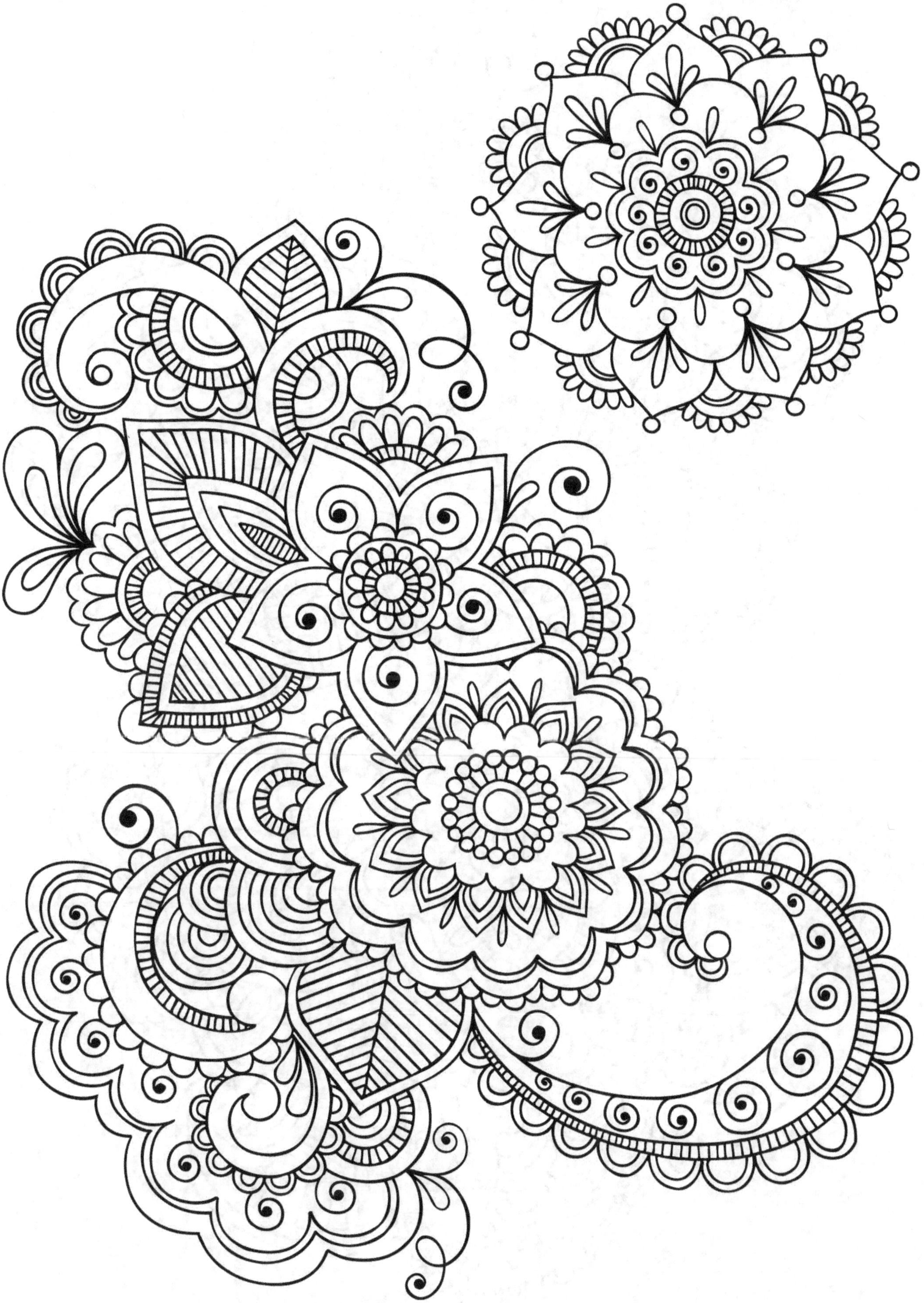

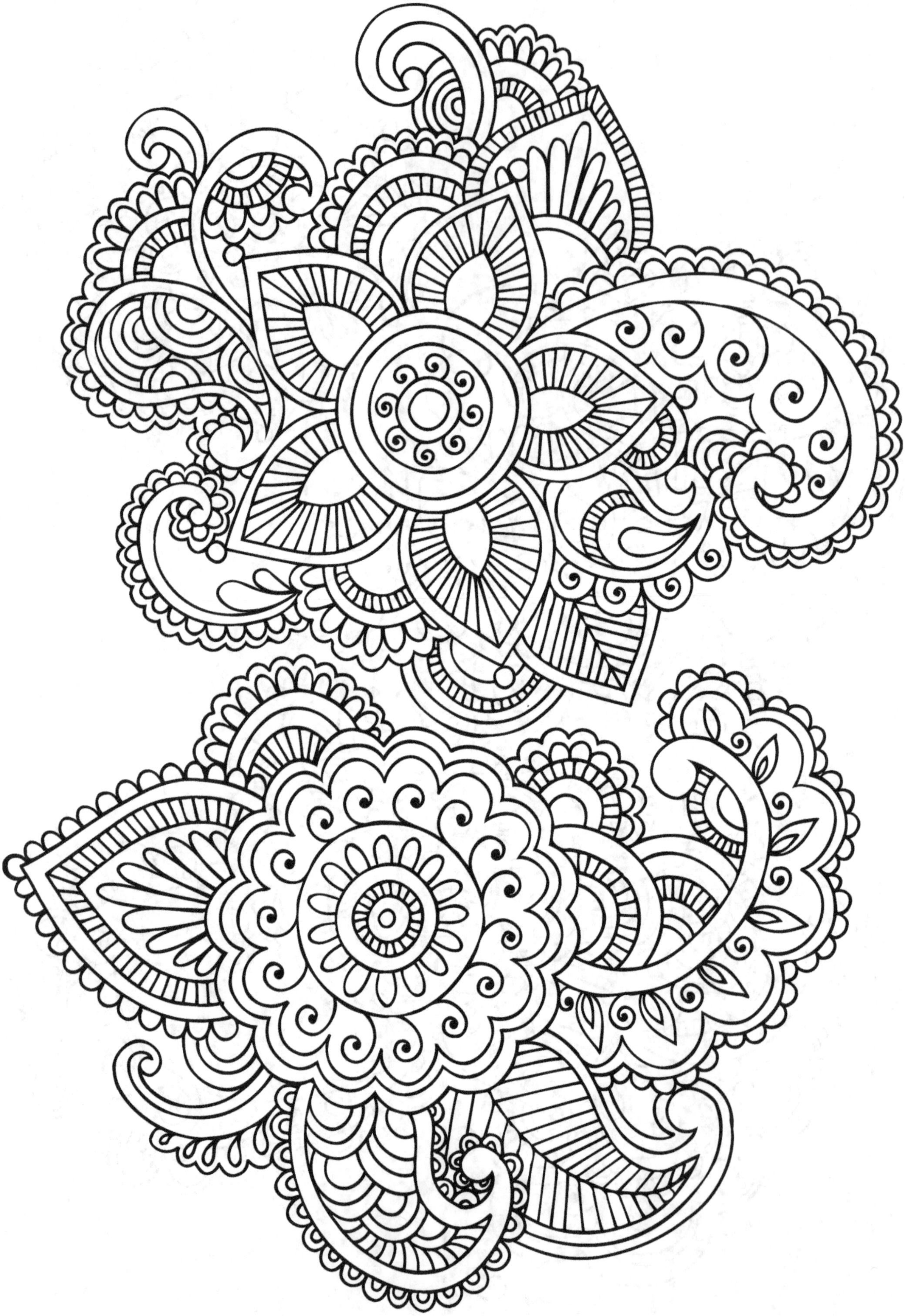

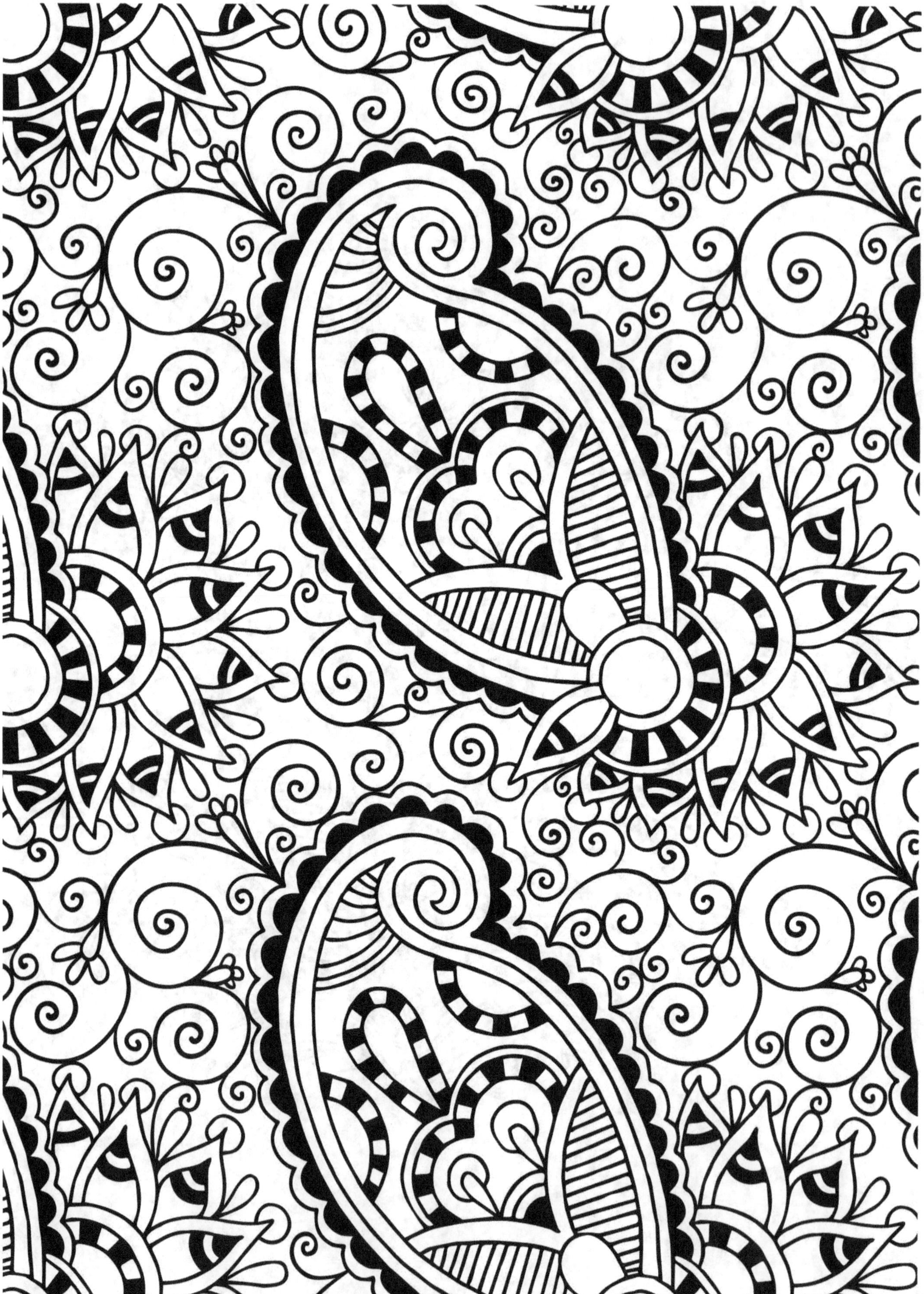

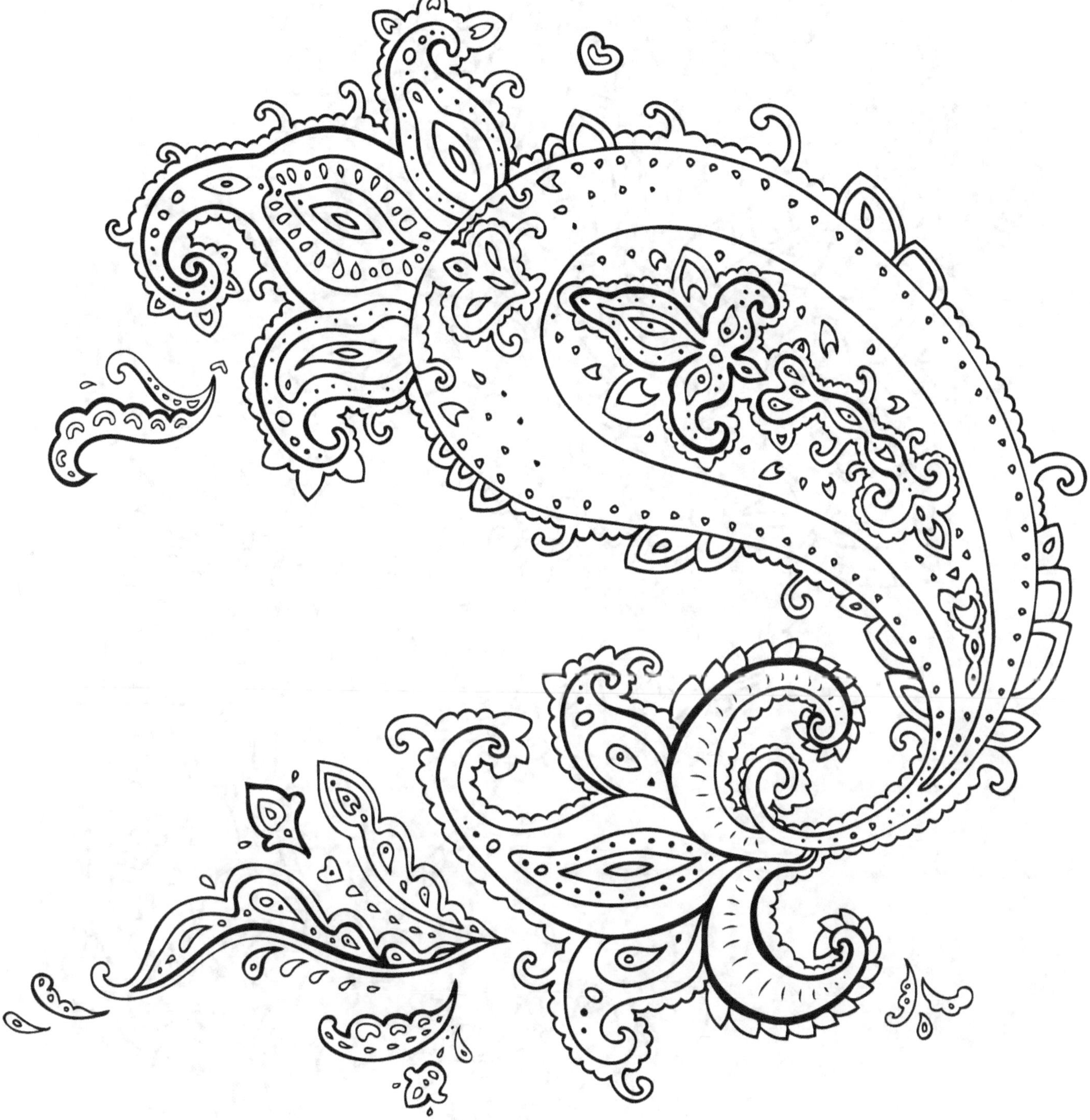

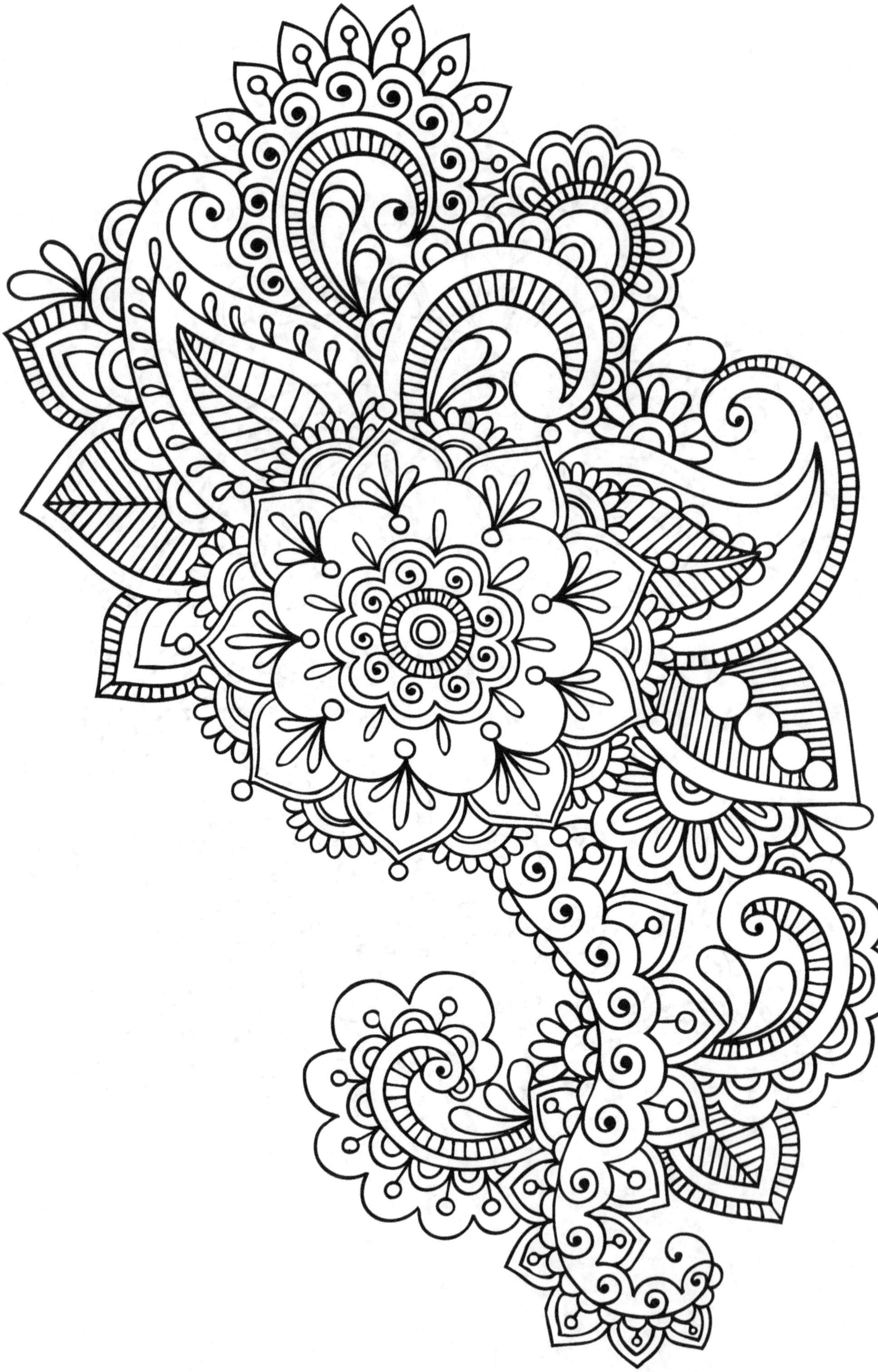

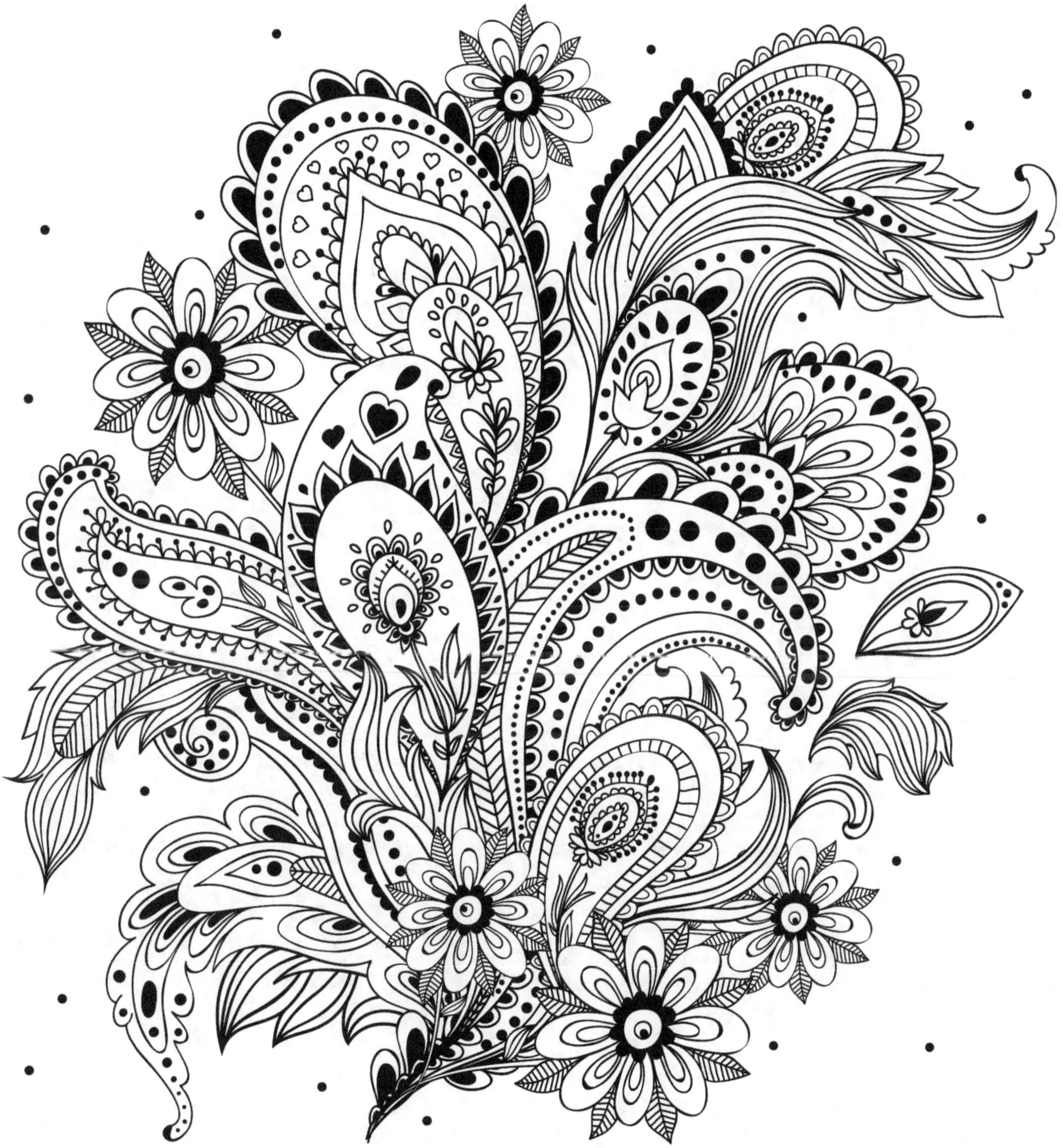

www.ingramcontent.com/pod-product-compliance
Lightning Source LLC
Chambersburg PA
CBHW080917290526
45795CB00007BA/2558
* 9 7 8 1 5 1 1 8 3 2 4 8 9 *